The ⭐⭐⭐⭐⭐ 5-STAR HOST

Soar From Subpar to Superstar and
Create a Steady Stream of 5-Star Reviews
for Your Short-Term Rental

By Catherine DeGeorge

The 5-Star Host © Copyright 2023 SPS Publishing. All rights reserved.

No part of this publication may be reproduced, distributed, or transmitted in any form or by any means, including photocopying, recording, or other electronic or mechanical methods, without the prior written permission of the publisher, except in the case of brief quotations embodied in critical reviews and certain other noncommercial uses permitted by copyright law.

Although the author and publisher have made every effort to ensure that the information in this book was correct at press time, the author and publisher do not assume and hereby disclaim any liability to any party for any loss, damage, or disruption caused by errors or omissions, whether such errors or omissions result from negligence, accident, or any other cause.

Adherence to all applicable laws and regulations, including international, federal, state and local governing professional licensing, business practices, advertising, and all other aspects of doing business in the US, Canada or any other jurisdiction is the sole responsibility of the reader and consumer.

Neither the author nor the publisher assumes any responsibility or liability whatsoever on behalf of the consumer or reader of this material. Any perceived slight of any individual or organization is purely unintentional.

ISBN (paperback): 979-8-88759-155-1

ISBN (eBook): 979-8-88759-156-8

READ THIS FIRST
GET YOUR FREE GIFT!

To get the best experience with this book, I've found readers who download and use the companion workbook are able to implement faster and take the next steps needed to gain a steady stream of 5-star reviews.

To say thanks for buying my book, I would like to give you a downloadable companion workbook 100% free!

Please download your free companion workbook at:

The5-StarHost.com/Workbook

DOWNLOAD THE COMPANION WORKBOOK FOR FREE!

WHAT IS YOUR 5-STAR REVIEW BLOCKER?

TAKE OUR FREE QUIZ!

Take this FREE 60-Second Quiz to find out what your 5-Star review blocker is. You'll receive a FREE REPORT explaining your unique results so you'll know which sections of this book to focus on first.

Take the quiz at:
5StarHostQuiz.com

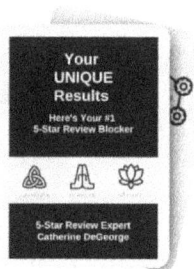

To get the best experience with this book, I've found readers who take this quiz and pinpoint their 5-Star Review Blocker are able to implement faster and take the next steps needed to gain a steady stream of 5-star reviews.

GET YOUR FREE REPORT NOW!

DEDICATION

I'm grateful for the wonderful places I've traveled to, and for all the companions I've shared life's adventures with, including:

My Parents

I dedicate this book to my parents, Richard and Fern, for always loving and supporting me and teaching me the value of education. Thank you for taking me to amazing places around the world and instilling the travel bug in me. (I think the dictionary and typewriter you gave me may have paid off.)

My Sisters

To my sisters, Anne Marie and Rebecca, I want to thank you for your encouragement, love, and support throughout our lives. Also, for being exemplary role models as well as fun playmates and travel companions. (Pancake me!)

My Husband

To my husband, Jim, thank you for pulling together so many details for our trips and for being a wonderful travel partner. I'm happy you have kept my travel bug alive, and I am grateful for every adventure with you. (Here's to completing our bucket list.)

ACKNOWLEDGMENTS

A huge heartfelt thank you to Jim, Rebecca, Guila, Anne Marie, Hannah, Grace, and Nathaniel for your contributions to the stories told in this book.

To My Readers

Thank you to all short-term rental hosts with the desire to raise above industry travel standards. Thank you for your hospitality and for giving us the time and attention to making our stays as memorable as possible. Our holidays and vacations wouldn't be as enjoyable if it weren't for you.

Table of Contents

Introduction 11
    The 5-Star Host'r Inception 18
Chapter 1: Monsoon to Movement. 21
    Review: Phoenix Baseball Tournament. 25
    Introducing The 5-Star Host'r Movement 26
    The 5-Star Host'r Way—<u>Target Your Micro-Niche</u> 27
SECTION 1 : SUBLETTING YOUR OWN HOME WHILE AWAY 35
Chapter 2: VRBOhhhhhh Noooooo. 37
    Review: Thanksgiving Condo in Lawrence. 43
    Key Takeaways and Design Hot Tips 43
    The 5-Star Host'r Way—<u>Communication</u> 44
    5-Star Host'r Action Plan. 52
Chapter 3: Air B & Beware. 53
    Review: Siesta Key Beach Bungalow 59
    Key Takeaways And Design Hot Tips 61
    The 5-Star Host'r Way—<u>Branding</u>. 62
    5-Star Host'r Action Plan. 69
Chapter 4: Instruction Overload 71
    Review: Thanksgiving House in Lawrence 77
    Key Takeaways And Design Hot Tips 77
    The 5-Star Host'r Way—<u>House Manual And Safety Tips</u> 79
    5-Star Host'r Action Plan. 87
SECTION 2: RENTING OUT THE ENTIRE HOUSE 89
Chapter 5: Booking Bare Minimum 91
    Review: North Carolina Beach House 96
    Key Takeaways And Design Hot Tips 97
    The 5-Star Host'r Way—<u>Essentials Per Room</u> 97

>   5-Star Host'r Action Plan.................................. 101
> Chapter 6: Someone Got It Right!........................ 103
>   Review: Siesta Key (2nd Stay)......................... 106
>   Key Takeaways And Design Hot Tips................... 106
>   The 5-Star Host'r Way—Alluring Amenities.............. 107
>   5-Star Host'r Action Plan.................................. 117
> Chapter 7: Price Gouging With A Twist.................... 119
>   Review: Stanford Graduation (Family Home)............. 126
>   Key Takeaways And Design Hot Tips................... 126
>   The 5-Star Host'r Way—Diversifying OTAs.............. 127
>   5-Star Host'r Action Plan.................................. 142
> **SECTION 3: RENTING SMALL SPACES................... 143**
> Chapter 8: Mayhem In Milan............................... 145
>   Review: Spain Single Room in Shared Home............. 147
>   Key Takeaways And Design Hot Tips................... 147
>   The 5-Star Host'r Way—Elevated Guest Experience....... 148
>   5-Star Host'r Action Plan.................................. 153
> Chapter 9: Sensory Overwhelm............................. 155
>   Review: Stanford Graduation Space Over Garage......... 159
>   Key Takeaways And Design Hot Tips................... 160
>   The 5-Star Host'r Way—Cleaning And Sensory Tips....... 162
>   5-Star Host'r Action Plan.................................. 167
> Chapter 10: Simple Splendor............................... 169
>   Review: Stanford Cottage/Bungalow.................... 172
>   Key Takeaways And Design Hot Tips................... 173
>   The 5-Star Host'r Way—Design And Styling............. 173
>   5-Star Host'r Action Plan.................................. 187
> Chapter 11: Conclusion................................... 189
>   The 5-Star Host'r Principles........................... 191
> Acronym Glossary....................................... 195

Introduction

Have you ever seen the movie, *The Holiday*?

If you haven't seen it, this romantic comedy stars Kate Winslet and Cameron Diaz as Iris and Amanda, two forsaken women from opposite sides of the ocean who arrange a home exchange to escape anguish during the holiday season.

Here is how that "home exchange" scene plays out:

Iris and Amanda, 6,000 miles apart, are in the same place—both, at a low point from bad breakups.

> Amanda Googles: "Where do I want to go, by myself, depressed, at Christmas?"
>
> And was surprised to have the site *Home Exchange* come up.
>
> She finds Iris's cottage in England and messages her, "I'm interested in renting your house. Is it still available? If it is, you could be a real lifesaver. I know it's late to be asking... but if you're at all interested, please contact me."
>
> Iris replies, "I'm very interested, but the cottage is only available for home exchange."
>
> Amanda asks, "Home exchange, what is that?"

Iris answers, "We switch houses, cars, everything. I haven't done it before, but friends of mine have." Then, she asks, "Where are you?" while whispering under her breath, *please say somewhere far away.*

When she finds out it is L.A., she replies, "I've never been there, but I've always wanted to go. I'm Iris by the way. Very normal. Neat freak. Healthy. Non-smoker. Single." (as she begins to cry)

Amanda introduces herself, "I'm Amanda. Loner, loser and complicated wreck."

Followed by, "Must say, your house looks idyllic. Just what I need."

Iris replies, "Really? Thanks. What does your place look like?"

Amanda: "My place is nice—a little bigger than yours."

Iris: *Not hard to be.*

After a few more exchanges (I don't want to give the movie away if you haven't seen it), Amanda asks, "When can I come?"

Iris responds, "Tomorrow too soon???"

Amanda thinks about it and replies, "Tomorrow's perfect!"

And so they agree that they will exchange houses for two weeks—starting the very next day.

I'm guessing you're wondering at this point, why I am bringing this up.

Well, you may think I'm crazy, but I have a theory.

I am convinced that the movie *The Holiday*, which premiered in 2006, is what led to the inception of Airbnb, only one and a half years later!

To explain my rationale, here is the timeline:

INTRODUCTION

According to Wikipedia, Airbnb was founded and launched in August 2008 in San Francisco, California, because the founders realized that travelers had difficulty finding lodging in the city during an Industrial Design Conference. That's just a year and a half after the movie launched.

Coincidence? Only the owners know for sure, but soon thereafter, Airbnb took off like wildfire and so began the short-term rental (STR) business where anyone could take advantage of bringing in some quick side cash by renting out their space.

Fast forward to today, and we see that the Airbnb platform alone has over 150 million users and hosts more than half a billion guests per year. Here's a quick look at Airbnb's user base and demographics:

- There are over 7 million active listings worldwide
- Airbnb has listings in over 220 countries and regions
- There are 4 million hosts worldwide on Airbnb
- 14,000 new hosts are joining the platform each month in 2022
- Six guests check into an Airbnb listing every second
- Over 1 billion guests have stayed at an Airbnb
- Airbnb listings make up 19% of the total demand for lodging in the U.S.

VRBO has also been dominating the STR travel industry and is one of Airbnb's biggest competitors. There are more than 2 million listings on VRBO, and the platform operates in 190 countries.

In fact, STR portals such as Airbnb, VRBO, Booking.com, Homestay, Expedia, and the like have changed the way people travel, and trends continue to evolve despite the ever-changing landscape of travel restrictions and dwelling regulations.

But back to Iris and Amanda… imagine what they must've been thinking. Think of how risky that was to go to a foreign country and exchange homes with a total stranger. They must've been crazy to have such deep faith in each other.

Just think about all the things that could have gone wrong.

And it's feasible that this is what the owners of Airbnb also thought when developing their travel portal—because it's hard to know who to trust, without a way to verify reliability and quality.

Enter… Reviews!

Prior to the Internet, word-of-mouth always played a major role when it came to the credibility of a business. However, online reviews now seem to carry as much weight as a personal recommendation from someone you know.

As trustpilot.com points out, "reviews open up a world of possibilities. They help consumers make smarter choices and are instrumental to improving companies."

They say that "in a world filled with decisions, reviews offer simple, relevant guidance. Decisions, even minor ones, can be difficult and tiresome, particularly when we're presented with so many options. Humans can only process so much information at once."

According to research conducted by Fan & Fuel, 97 percent of participants said customer reviews factor into their buying decisions. And 92 percent of consumers hesitate to purchase when there are no customer reviews.

They go on to say:

- 79% of customers put as much weight on online reviews as they would on personal recommendations
- On average, reviews produce an 18% uplift in sales
- 86% of people hesitate to do business with a company if it has negative online reviews

Statistics from bigcommerce.com indicate that "in today's web-based world, 91% of people read reviews, and 84% trust them as much as they would a personal recommendation."

They mention the following top three benefits of positive reviews:

1. Drive Sales

   In essence, people want proof from other consumers that a product or service is worthwhile, not just biased advertising from brands. In fact, reviews are trusted 12 times more than other marketing materials.

2. Build Trust

   Social proof refers to the psychological phenomenon in which people make judgments and decisions based on the collective actions of others.

   Customers are 63 percent more likely to trust and buy from a company with good reviews.

3. Aid Customer Decision-Making

   When purchasing online, the customer decision-making process becomes a lot more complicated. As such, most shoppers put a lot more time and energy into evaluating products, reading reviews, and comparing items with one another before pulling the trigger.

   An astounding 94 percent of online consumers have been dissuaded from booking based on negative reviews, so remedying the problematic reviews can definitely be beneficial.

How does this relate to the travel industry?

These benefits transfer over to the travel industry as well. In fact, Airbnb has come up with its own way to make the review process more profitable, and that is with its "Superhost" category.

But how exactly do reviews influence STR booking decisions?

According to Airdna.com, hosts earn significantly more revenue on Airbnb when they receive the Superhost stamp of approval. They state that the uptick in STR booking decisions can be seen in these key performance indicators:

- They experience an 81% higher occupancy rate
- They earn 60% more revenue per available day

- And they see a 5% improvement in listing traffic

VRBO also states the importance of reviews on their portal:

- If potential guests find a glowing review, they're much more likely to hit "book."
- What's more, positive reviews on VRBO will increase a property's position in search results, helping it stand out from competitors.

  In other words, 5-star reviews can help place your listing position on page one of a potential guest's search—versus pages two to ten, which few people search through—and can bump the property's position closer to the top of that search page.

So, by now, you have a good understanding of all the benefits of reviews and why striving for 5-star reviews is so important for your STR.

But you may wonder, "What is the biggest reason why hosts are *not* receiving those coveted 5-star reviews?"

Here is the truth: Hosting an STR is a "business" and needs to be treated like one. You can't just expect to post an ad on one of the travel platforms and start hosting guests without having a plan laid out first. Think of it like building a house; that plan needs to start with a solid foundation.

You see, most people seem worried about making a quick buck, like putting as many "heads in beds" that they can fit. But these trends do not lead to a profitable long-term business. Nor does this fad bring consistent 5-star reviews.

I mean, who wants to sleep in a blow-up bed in an overcrowded space on vacation? I sure don't.

If you want to become a 5-star STR host, you need to change how you're doing things. Stop listening to all the gurus telling you how to improve your SEO with tricks such as changing out photos daily and trying to manipulate the system and the algorithms.

The online consumer has become too sophisticated for such trickery.

Instead, make it a "People Business" and focus on not only meeting needs, but exceeding expectations.

You need to get out of the logistics and into what really matters. STRs should be all about *hospitality*, and many hosts forget that.

Shouldn't the host's goal be to cater to the guest in order to get rave reviews, referrals, and repeat customers? The answer is a resounding YES. Reviews should be the number one focus for any STR host.

But if you're not a business, marketing, and hospitality expert, then where do you begin?

Let me show you how…

You see, I come from the hospitality industry, and I was an interior designer hired specifically to design hotels that drew in their clientele. The secrets I learned along the way will help you as an STR host take the best strategies, remove the subpar techniques, and transfer those proprietary tips to your hosting business.

But what makes my viewpoint unique?

Not only am I an interior design grad with hospitality design experience, but I am also an Airbnb super guest turned STR design expert. Through the years, I've sifted through thousands of STR listings to select the best options of where to stay on our journeys and what I have learned is that most people are not doing it right.

But who can blame them? It's completely understandable. Most hosts have not spent years studying hospitality, design and marketing. That can take decades to learn.

So why not learn from someone who is an expert in all of these areas and shortcut your way to success?

Who is this book for?

If you're just starting out in the STR arena or are a seasoned host seeking better reviews; whether you are subletting your own home while you're away, renting an entire house, or renting a small space, then you are in the right place.

The stories throughout this book will teach you how to do things the right way in order to gain a steady stream of 5-star reviews.

This book is not for Superhosts with consistent 5-Star reviews—although you may still find a few gold nuggets throughout this book that you hadn't already thought of or implemented.

After all, in Chapter 3 of this book, I describe a not-so-wonderful experience at a Superhost's property. So there is always room for improvement.

Are you tired of sleepless nights wondering why you aren't receiving more bookings, more revenue and more 5-star reviews?

Are you fed up with trying to figure out the right strategies to get consistent 5-star reviews for your STR?

Then you are in the right place.

I am on a mission to improve on the STR Industry. My goal is to change the landscape of subpar stays and reviews. I believe that every STR host has the ability to become a 5-Star Host by following the hospitality tips I suggest throughout this book.

In fact, I am so passionate about this mission that I trademarked the term the **"5-Star Host'r."**™

The 5-Star Host'r sets higher standards than the average host, to provide their guests the best experience possible.

It's all about stepping up your game and setting higher standards. Think of it as supersizing.

The term 5-Star Host'r encompasses any STR host striving to get a steady stream of 5-star reviews, no matter which online travel agency (OTA) you choose to advertise on or if you have a direct booking site—more on this in Chapter 7.

You will learn that it is not necessary to spend a fortune, or become a luxury accommodation, to achieve this. Any type of STR property, in any price range, in any location can benefit from implementing the lessons in this book.

INTRODUCTION

This book helps you up the ante and raise the bar from where you currently are. It is about standing out from the masses and stopping the scroll.

It's about evolving your hospitality, your design, and your marketing to the 5-Star Host'r level.

It's time to learn how to do things the right way to get true rankings that will stick and raise you to the top of searches simply because "You Are That Good!"

Leave your old beliefs behind, and I'll show you the way through targeting, design, and hospitality. Learn to do it the right way. You'll be thrilled with your results.

Throughout this book, I will tell you stories of my family's experiences and my experiences at STRs. I will tell you about the good, the bad and the ugly. I will tell you the rating each stay was given and why.

Then, I will dissect the key takeaways and design tips from that stay, followed by a section titled "The 5-Star Host'r Way," which will tell you how to take those lessons one step further to rise above your competition.

Don't be the kind of person who misses out on a great opportunity because you are trying one new trend after the other and not seeing the results you know you should be getting. Be the kind of person that others admire. Be the kind of person other people see and wonder, "how do they do it?"

> Margaret, a host from Arizona, says, "The best thing about this book is that it is easy to comprehend and has actionable steps so that it can be read on Sunday, and within just one week after implementing the ideas you're already noticing the results."

I promise that if you follow the steps I've outlined in this book, you'll see a steady stream of 5-Star reviews moving forward like Margaret did. This, in turn, will increase your rankings and placement on the

Internet and on the various OTAs, which will drive more traffic to your listing.

The hospitality tips and techniques you are about to read have been proven to create positive results and 5-star reviews. I encourage you to be an action taker and implementer. All you have to do to become a 5-Star Host'r is to keep reading.

Are you ready to join the ranks of the 5-Star Host'rs?

Chapter 1

Monsoon to Movement

It was early October when my husband and I awakened to the sound of battering rain. Not so unusual, but we were in Phoenix, Arizona.

Wait, what?? Rain in Arizona??

We had arrived late the night before and were excited to attend day one of my husband's baseball tournament. But little did we know that the monsoon season hit late this particular year, and unfortunately, we were homebound for the day.

Luckily, we had both brought our laptops, knowing we would have some daily work to complete during the five-day stay.

As we looked around the condo we had rented for the week, we realized the condo offered no good places to set up a workstation for either of us.

I spotted the high-top kitchen table and claimed my perch on a clunky barstool. The fact that my laptop cord did not reach any nearby outlets was only the first of many annoyances to come.

Couldn't this host have picked a chair that was actually comfortable to sit in, I thought? I know that if she had tried sitting in this chair to eat a meal, she would've realized that although they may have completed a "look" she was attempting to create, they were terribly uncomfortable.

After searching for the proper light switch for over five minutes, I settled in to begin working. Yet I felt the space was not well lit to work, and then I realized that half of the light bulbs in the chandelier over the table were burned out.

Ok, I could deal with these minor inconveniences, I suppose. But then I realized that I did not have the password to her Internet.

I searched and searched for any type of House Manual or any notes lying around that would provide the login info I was searching for. I even looked at all the various magnets she had all over the refrigerator and still came up empty-handed.

My remaining option was to call the host and get it from her. But, you guessed it, she did not answer her phone.

Meanwhile, my husband decided that the only place for him to set up his laptop was on the sofa. The rain began beating heavier now, pounding on the roof. As darkness crept across the room, he struggled to find a nearby outlet, but there were zero light sources nearby, so he was basically fumbling about in a dark room.

Since we couldn't access the Internet to do our work, we decided to turn on the TV. Wow, was that a mistake!

We spent half an hour locating what we thought was the TV remote control, only to find out that it controlled the overhead fan.

At this point, we were starting to get a bit frustrated. What could we do to fill our time on this rainy day?

We decided to go to the grocery store to buy ingredients for a tasty homecooked meal that night. I mean, after all, isn't this why Airbnb has become so popular? People want the comforts of their own home, and cooking a meal is a part of that.

As we entered the grocery store, we noticed buckets on every aisle. Apparently, they were there to collect the rain seeping through the roof. I had never seen anything like this. But my husband reminded me that they rarely get rain in Phoenix, let alone these heavy monsoons that drop buckets of rain in a short amount of time onto a seriously sun-beaten roof. Therefore, they were unaware the roof was in disrepair until a monsoon hit. I shook my head and chuckled!

Returning to our condo from the grocery store was quite a feat, as the roads were flooding, but we managed to return safely. As we leaped over rivers of rushing water to get back to our condo, our shoes became instantly soaked all the way through. Slosh, slosh, slosh! That's never fun!

But now, we had a more serious issue at hand than our soggy shoes. Bags in tow, we struggled to open the combo lock on the front door. Here we were, standing in the pouring rain, and the combo code that had worked for us just the night before was now suddenly giving us an *error* code. Geez!

We tried to call the host again, and fortunately, this time, she answered. She said the one-time code she had set for us must have shut off early and that she could not reset it for us by phone. She recommended that we go four doors down and get a key from the neighbor to let us in.

That did not make us feel very comfortable. The neighbor had a key to get into our condo? We had valuables in there. Was he to be trusted?

Nonetheless, we reluctantly knocked on his door, and he willingly gave us his spare key. Thank goodness he was home, and he was very kind.

We were relieved that the key worked, and once inside the condo, we removed our drenched clothes and shoes and changed into dry clothing. On a good note, I was pleased to see that the host had left laundry soap, so I could wash our soiled clothes.

Then, I realized that during the rain deluge, we forgot to ask the host for the Internet login. So I called her again, and she sheepishly apologized that she had not provided it to us. Once we had that established, I asked her where the TV remote was located; sadly, she had no idea. She said the previous guests must've misplaced it. Great, that was no help to us!

Oh well, at least now we could get some work done and could watch movies from our computers.

Not so much! I don't know if it was the stormy weather or just bad service, but the Internet could not hold a connection for more than ten minutes at a time.

Irritated beyond belief now, we decided to start preparing our dinner. We had decided on tacos since they seemed easy to make in someone else's kitchen. But we couldn't even find a cutting board or sharp knife to cut our tomatoes. And if there was no cutting board, do you think she had a cheese grater? Of course not.

So, after all of this frustration, we decided to change course and called some of my husband's teammates to meet them out for dinner. *Maybe we could end this miserable day on a good note,* we thought.

During dinner, we discussed our accommodations with each other, and we found out that most of them had booked rooms at a nearby hotel. Their experiences were drastically different than ours. No complaints at all.

Some had spent the day working seamlessly, while others watched movies all afternoon to kill time.

I was starting to regret having booked this STR versus a hotel room like the rest of the gang had. But we honestly believed the property description she had provided on Airbnb that stated her place had "plenty of light and ample space to work," and she even boasted that she had all the TV channels one could ever dream of. Not so much!

Day three arrived, and it was still raining. This trip was turning into a disastrous vacation, and we were ready to get the heck out of there. The drudgery of our daily work seemed to linger on and on. We were upset that we had spent so much money on the trip, and it seemed pointless since my husband hadn't even played one baseball game yet.

Finally, on day four, the rain stopped. The tournament was back on, but now they would have to play all of their games in two days rather than spread out through the original five days. That's a LOT of games!

Can you say, "sore muscles?" These poor guys. That's a lot of games to play for any age, let alone the 50-year-old's league.

My husband tried to look at the bright side and pointed out that at least he could soak his achy muscles in the condo's hot tub later that evening.

Excited about the relaxing evening we had in store, we grabbed our towels and some cocktails and headed out. Dismally, we learned that the hot tub was not working properly. The water was lukewarm, and the heater was not working, nor were the jets. Are you kidding me?

This was no longer frustrating; it was an outrage. "Don't people know how to run a proper Airbnb? It's not that hard!" I exclaimed.

In my fury, I started thinking about how many STRs we'd stayed in and all the disappointments we'd had along the way—many of which you will read about in this book.

I don't want to condemn every STR host because many people do a great job and certainly deserve a 5-star review. But I have tale after tale of subpar stays, like when we went to Tucson for a spring baseball tournament and the pool they advertised—which was my number one criteria for booking—was closed for repairs.

Or the time we rented a condo in Hawaii but arrived to find our ocean view room was, in fact, a room looking out to the condo across the way.

As I analyzed our less-than-desirable stays, the main theme noticed through all these travel experiences is that very few hosts seemed to know what they were doing.

Some hosts got a few things right but lacked in other areas, while some just seemed to throw up a listing willy-nilly with no idea of what they were doing. Then, I realized that throughout all of our years of traveling, we have only had one repeat STR stay, which I'll tell you about later, and that's because nobody else was doing it at a level that would make us want to return.

Then, it dawned on me… I realized that I had the knowledge that could help STR hosts do a better job and that is the moment I decided to do what I could to change things.

Introducing…

THE 5-STAR HOST'R MOVEMENT

At its core, the 5-Star Host'r Movement is all about hosting with purpose. It's about putting the guest at the center of every decision. It's about discovering the areas for improvement and finding simple but effective ways to enhance your guest's stay. It's about raising the standards to stand out from your competition.

Selfishly, I just want better accommodation while experiencing the area like a local. I want to travel knowing that I will have the ease of checking in, as I do at a hotel. I want to have the comforts of home. I want the experiences of a tourist. I want all of this wrapped up with one pretty bow. And I know that I'm not the only one with this desire.

I don't want to endure some of the mishaps, hiccups, and miscommunication, as seen throughout some of the stories I'll tell you. I want simple comfort. And I don't think that's too much to ask.

But this benefits you as well…

I want to take all I have learned in the last three decades about hospitality, design, and marketing and pass it on to you. I want to shortcut your way to success. I want you to rise above the crowd and become that listing that stops the scroll.

I want to show you how to rise above the industry standards and really shine.

I want to make your job easier. I want you to experience the joy of rave reviews, nonstop referrals, and repeat guests. There's beauty in that.

Are you ready to up the ante?

Let's get started…

THE 5-STAR HOST'R WAY—TARGET YOUR MICRO-NICHE

As you well know, this industry is growing exponentially. The truth is this industry has grown so quickly that it is getting harder and harder to stand out from the crowd.

As more and more travelers—singles, couples, families and business people—discover the advantages that a STR property offers over staying in a traditional hotel, more and more people will seriously consider becoming an STR host. You will need to find a way to stand out.

So, the million-dollar question at this point is, "How do you go about getting your listing to stand out above all of the competition and more importantly, how do you get consistent 5-star reviews"?

The majority of STRs that my family and I have stayed at seem as if they don't have a purpose. They are available for rent to anyone and everyone who is a paying customer.

But those who try to be everything to everyone end up being nothing to anyone!

Fact: You will actually attract fewer people if you are trying to attract everyone; therefore, you need to become highly specific in who your ideal guest is.

And that brings me to lesson #1 of becoming a 5-Star Host'r.

Targeting Your Ideal Guest

If you don't know specifically "who" you are serving, anything you come up with is a guess because you are basically trying to serve everyone.

Targeting your ideal guest is at the core of your foundation. Once you have targeted your ideal guest, you can create offers they want, and all other decisions will be built on top of this.

This is what the most successful hotels in the world do.

Think about it—they all have their own niche or ideal guest they are targeting, and everything they do revolves around that particular type of guest.

For instance, some hotel brands are known for their price point, some for the amenities they offer, and some for the type of travelers, such as families, adventurers, or executives. Yet others focus on the ease of the traveler and are located off the highway or right by an airport.

Take, for example, some of the newcomers to the market who have their own unique way of differentiating themselves from the competition:

- The Great Wolf Lodge caters to families with children who like adventure. Their centerpiece attraction is the expansive indoor water park, which is for resort guests only, and admission to the water park is included in the room rate. Great Wolf Lodge offers an easy and unforgettable way to stay and play for families. Their slogan is, "Stay as a pack, dream as a pack." And recent ads are running with the following slogan, "Nothing brings the pack together like Great Wolf Lodge."

  What a great concept! I would've begged and pleaded with my parents to go here when I was a child if this place had been around.

- The Hyatt Zilara and Ziva are all-inclusive resorts—meaning you can expect food, drinks, activities, and entertainment to be included in the price of your accommodation without having to pay extra for it. These resorts offer countless opportunities to enjoy life. While Hyatt Ziva offers fun for guests of all ages, Hyatt Zilara is adults-only.

  My husband and I have gone to these and absolutely love the all-inclusive concept. We enjoy these resorts so much that we rarely leave the resort for any off-site activities. They have thought of everything right there, so why leave? It's a trip in and of itself.

If we follow the proven steps of the hotel industry, it becomes evident that your starting point is choosing your ideal guest and basing your lodging, essentials, concierge services, amenities, design, and marketing around this. Every decision you make and everything you do must build upon that foundation.

In other words, it is imperative that you become guest-centric, focusing everything on that ideal guest rather than money-centric, focusing solely on your profits.

But the 5-Star Host'r Way advises taking that guest-centric theory one step further.

I'm betting you've heard the phrase, "the riches are in the niches," but that no longer works in this overcrowded STR market.

You now need to pinpoint a "micro-niche." You need to narrow down your category further from ideal guest to targeted ideal guest; I'll refer to this as "TIG" for the remainder of the book.

For example, if your ideal guest category is families, you need to narrow that down further to specify if your property caters to and is set up for babies and toddlers. If you allow the family pet to come, or if your property is set up for the senior or elderly family members to join along, those are examples of a family micro-niche.

Go smaller to go bigger. This journey will take you from where you are to where you want to go.

Instead of asking "What," you must ask, "Who should I serve." It's the single most important decision to become a 5-Star Host'r.

The "what" will come once you know the "who." In turn, this will provide your unique angle in an oversaturated market.

Moving forward, it will take the uncertainty out of everything you are putting your time, money, and energy into.

It's all about being guest-centric, or in the 5-Star Host'rs case, it's about being *TIG-centric*.

"Why," you ask?

Because once you position yourself with your TIG in mind:

- 5-star reviews will follow
- Return guests will follow
- A steady flow of TIG bookings will follow
- A steady revenue flow will follow
- Easy targeted marketing will follow
- Easy design decisions will follow
- Easy amenity selections will follow
- You will become a 5-Star Host'r!

Everything will come together like a well-orchestrated symphony when you implement this lesson.

Let's Discover Your TIG

Whether you are just starting out or if you are a seasoned STR host, I promise this exercise will help you.

I want you to picture a bullseye, like a dart board. Now imagine throwing a dart and hitting the center target.

Bullseye/Center Target = Your TIG.

Shooting for the center target is how you will narrow down from your ideal guest to your TIG. As each circle gets smaller, we gain a better understanding of who that person is.

Grab a pen and paper and write down the answers to the following questions in order to get a better understanding of exactly who your ideal guest is. You might even know an actual person who matches this description.

I'm going to show you how to pinpoint your ideal guest and encompass your entire STR around that avatar.

Let's start narrowing down to find the perfect person who needs the space you are renting.

1. Check Out the Competition

First, do a little research to understand your market and who your competition is. Spend some time surveying the market for your competition, including hotels, and see if they have a noticeable brand and what they offer to their guests.

2. Research Trends

Keep an eye on the news to discover local events or trends that can help or hurt your bookings. Is there an upcoming festival or sporting event you can mention to draw in more interest? Is there a popular item guests are drawn to that can help you stand out?

3. Review Statistics (From Airbnb)

- 60% of Airbnb's users are millennials
- 54% of guests that book through Airbnb are female
- 36% of Airbnb guests are between 25-34 years old
- 15% of guests are 18-24 years old
- 13% of guests are 55+ years old
- 88% of bookings are for 2-4 guests (most needed)

4. Review Demographics of Property

Understand that each STR is unique. Sometimes, you can decide what type of STR you're going to create and other times, it's decided for you based on the following:

A. Geographic Area

- Would your property be considered a vacation rental or destination? Examples might include a lakefront or beach property, a mountain property, or a property in a scenic or tourist area.
- Is your property located in a city where you would cater to the executive or business traveler?
- Would travelers come to your location for conferences or big events?
- Would people come to your location for an off-the-grid experience? Examples might include no Wi-Fi or limited amenities.

B. Location of Property

- Is it close to downtown or in an area with no hotels?
- Is there a great restaurant within walking distance?
- Are you near a beautiful park to explore?
- Is your property located near an airport, highway, or tourist area?
- What is in your area that would attract STR guests? Examples might include traveling for work, vacation, local events, or attractions.

C. Size and Type of Property

- How many guests are allowed comfortably in real beds, not blow-ups?
- Is your property suited for extended families?

- Are you set up for families with babies or young children?
- Are you set up for seniors and the elderly?
- Are pets allowed?

D. Characteristics of Property

- Does your property include a kitchen with a stove, sink, and refrigerator?
- Does your property include laundry facilities?
- Is your property large enough for entertaining?
- Does your house have a great backyard for gatherings?
- Is your property in an HOA with special amenities available to guests?

5. Identify the Demographics of Your Ideal Guest

- What type of person will travel to your area?
- Describe this person's age, gender, education, income, relationship status, and family status.
- What makes this person tick, and what is important to this person? What are their hobbies?
- How do they spend their time—raising kids, working, adventure seeking, vacationing?
- What do their social media posts gravitate toward—beachcomber, mountain dweller, business executive, or family-oriented?

6. Diversify Services

- Would you consider leveraging guests to mid-term stays—over 30 days?
- Are you ADA-approved for handicapped or elderly?
- Are you optimized for the business traveler? Airbnb has a special category for this.

- Can you add in any unique experiences?

The key lesson here is to drill down from the larger niche markets to your micro-niche and to realize that you don't have to be everything to everyone.

You need to reach for that target, your bullseye. The more you can identify your TIG, the bigger your potential. Don't serve everyone. Repel those you don't want to rent to.

The more specific you narrow down to this TIG, the more bookings you will receive.

I promise, this journey will take you from where you are, to where you want to go.

Everything you do from beginning to end will be purpose-driven with your TIG in mind.

After determining who your TIG is, you can give your property a purpose and build everything around that.

You can start planning out things like what that guest will need during their stay. You'll be able to market your property with a particular audience in mind.

No more endless testing of the newest fads like heads in beds, arbitrage, or beating the latest algorithms. These all have their purpose, but they aren't getting the big picture.

Every decision, selection, and choice you make moving forward will be purpose-driven based on your TIG.

In this overcrowded space, you can no longer just be a guest-centric host. You now need to be TIG-centric to stand out in the crowd and rise above your competition.

Mission: My mission is to build a tribe of TIG-centric hosts and to make purpose-driven hosting the new norm.

I encourage you to implement this first step and get ready to join the 5-Star Host'r Movement!

SECTION 1
Subletting Your Own Home While Away

Many STR Hosts start out by renting their own homes while they leave for the week. Although this is a great way to test the waters to see if this is something you want to move forward with, as you'll see through the following chapters, it also presents many unnecessary problems for the guests.

If you want to do it the "right way," then follow my Key Takeaways and Design Hot Tips at the end of each chapter to avoid many common mistakes.

Make sure to absorb the information in the "5-Star Host'r Way" section. Each chapter contains a key lesson to focus on and implement into your business to sustain a steady stream of 5-star reviews.

Finally, be sure to implement the quick and easy steps at the end of each chapter because knowledge only gets you so far. It's in the implementation that brings success.

Chapter 2

VRBOhhhhhh Noooooo

If it wasn't one thing, it was another.

It was a crisp fall day, and my husband and I had just arrived at my dad's for our annual Thanksgiving week together. My family lives from one end of the country to the other, so we travel from all over and converge at his house in Kansas. The middle of the country. Yes, I know, you're thinking, "That must be boring," but not at all when you're with this crew.

As the years have passed, our family has grown, and we've expanded our crew with spouses and children, so we no longer fit comfortably in one house. Therefore, my sister and her spouse volunteer to stay in a nearby STR. That way, they have their own space to sleep and shower, but they join us during the days for all the family gatherings.

This particular year, my sister and her spouse found themselves delayed at the airport, so their flight arrived two hours late. When they landed in Kansas City, they were tired and hungry, but they persevered and jumped on the red bus to be taken to the building where they would pick up their rental car.

As they pulled off the rental car lot in their compact car, they breathed a sigh of relief as they were finally on the last stretch of their trip. They typed their arrival address into the GPS and were grateful to have the luxury of guided assistance.

The 5-Star Host

Things seemed to be falling into place, and they were starting to relax. But about twenty miles down the road, their check engine light flashed on. I mean, who rents a car and has an issue immediately? I suppose it happens more often than not. But little did they know that this issue was just the beginning forecast of what lay ahead for these two.

So, they stopped at the nearest automotive place that they could find to have their car checked out. The mechanic pointed out that the battery was getting low, but he did not find any immediate issues, so they decided to drive the additional twenty miles to get to Lawrence.

Their GPS guided them to the condo complex, where an iron gate greeted them. No surprise here. The VRBO host had given them instructions ahead of time on how to enter through this gate.

They pulled up to the code detector and punched in the code they were given. And nothing happened. They tried the code again and again, and nothing.

Since it was cold and raining out, they were hoping to stay in the car to remain dry, but it was starting to look like that may not be the case.

Maybe they had been given the wrong code, they thought. So, they tried calling the owner for assistance, but she did not answer, so their only option was to leave a voicemail.

At this point, all my sister could think to do was to get out and jump over the fence. She reasoned that maybe she could open the gate from the inside. So, she left the warmth of her car and proceeded out into the rain to climb over the fence.

Fortunately, her ingenuity worked. They were in!

And wouldn't you know, a few minutes after they drove through the gate, the owner called.

"You're having trouble getting in? The code is 5490*."

VRBOHHHHHH NOOOOOO

"What?" my sister shrieked. "There is a star at the end of the numeric code? You never told us that. Well, that makes all the difference in the world."

She hung up the phone and was starting to get annoyed. I mean, why would the owner assume that everyone would know to input a star at the end of the numeric code? Why wouldn't she have specified this in her instructions? Not everyone lives behind an iron gate and would know this as common knowledge.

Ok, deep breath. Time to let this go and park the car, she thought.

The parking lot was relatively small, and not being sure exactly where the condo unit was yet, they looked around and decided to park in the first empty spot they found.

Off they went in search of their condo with luggage in tow. At this point, it was too late to go to Dad's house, so they settled in for the night.

After a good night's sleep, they got up and went through their normal morning routine to get ready. They were excited to drive over to Dad's to see everyone and spend the day with us.

With anticipation, they walked out of the condo unit to their car but uh oh… their car was nowhere to be found.

They thought, *Were we that delirious when we arrived late last night that we can't remember where we parked?*

"Hmmm," they remarked, "that's odd." They searched and searched and still couldn't find it.

Despair was starting to set in. "Where is our car?"

They decided to call Dad to pick them up and bring them back to his house. This way, they could at least finally greet the family and deal with their newfound problem from his house.

After the enthusiastic hellos, they told us what had occurred and once again called the VRBO owner. They asked her if she knew what may have happened to their car, and she said she would check into it.

"Did she tell you which spot to park in?" we asked them.

"No," my sister answered, "I think she said there was a parking lot and to park outside of the unit. That's it. Nothing about a specific spot."

So, it turns out that although they did not have assigned parking spots in this condo development, everybody had a spot they normally parked in. And when a condo dweller arrived late at night and saw an unknown car in their regular allotted spot, they had it towed.

What??? Why would someone do that? My sister had no idea which spot was considered to be the "correct spot" for the condo unit they were renting. The owner had not offered any parking specifics. They simply parked in the first open spot they saw and thought nothing of it.

But now, they had a new dilemma—how to get their rental car back.

They spent the entire day figuring out where their car had been towed and how they would get it out of hock.

Who wants to spend an entire day out of a four-day vacation dealing with something like this? Certainly not I.

The following day, once the dust settled, they asked me to come over to their VRBO and give them my professional critique of the condo's interior. They were interested in seeing a designer's viewpoint of the space. This is something that I loved to do, so I jumped at the chance.

The first thing I noticed upon entry was that it had a very cold feeling. The furniture was old and did not look welcoming, and the finishes were all hard with no variety of textures.

The condo was an open layout so that once you stepped through the front door, you were in the living room that was open to the dining room and kitchen. The living room consisted of a huge jute rug; jute is a strong, coarse fiber used for making burlap.

I assumed the owner thought they were adding visual interest to the area, but they did not plan this with guests in mind because it felt tough and scratchy under-foot. It was also slick if the renter was

VRBOHHHHHH NOOOOOO

wearing slippers. It's an accident waiting to happen and a potential lawsuit in the making.

Surrounding this jute rug was a pair of old wooden chairs. They appeared to be antiques, but they were uncomfortable to sit in. Almost everything in this room had a hard surface, meaning voices and sounds echoed because there were very few soft surfaces to soften sounds.

Next, I noticed that there were odd accessories here and there. In particular, I remember a stack of old wooden suitcases piled on each other at different angles, topped with a stack of magazines. Was this supposed to be a clever accessory? An artistic highlight? To me, it was a stack of stuff waiting to be tipped over!! I'm sure, not what the owner was trying to present.

Across from the chairs was a small clunky sofa filled with a large variety of throw pillows—the only soft goods in the room. Not only did they not coordinate with anything, but because the sofa was so small, there was no room to sit on it unless you tossed all the pillows on the floor.

Then we moved into the kitchen, and I noticed that the doors of the cabinets had been removed. I mean, some kitchen cabinet makers actually design cabinets with no doors, to show off plates or glass collections. But this was nothing like that.

It was obvious the door fronts were purposefully removed but inside the cabinets was quite a mess of various food staples and mismatched dishware piled up. It was more of an eyesore than anything.

Moving into the bedroom, I noticed the exorbitant amount of throw pillows on the bed. The fabrics did not go with anything in the room and were aesthetically unappealing, but worse, you had nowhere to put all of these throw pillows when you wanted to sleep. They would have to be tossed on the floor with hopes that you would not trip over them and fall in the middle of the night. But if you put the pillows on the floor, you'd have no room for your luggage.

As we discussed my thoughts on the matter, my sister noted, "Sometimes people have multiple layers of pillows on STR beds, and you can't use any of them. You know, you're desperately looking for the one that feels good, but they're all decorative and behind those are the ones with big shams on them that you can't use either. And finally, you locate the pillows to sleep on, and you're just hoping they're good pillows. That's one thing that's really important to us is to have a good pillow because a really bad pillow can ruin your night."

I agreed but pointed out that people have different tastes and prefer all different styles. We handled that when I was designing hotels by ordering a variety of different thicknesses and firmness of pillows to sleep on. This way, a hotel guest could find what suited them best and could use as few or as many pillows as they wanted.

The final thing that stood out with the home's décor was that you would find some sort of Jayhawk or KU memorabilia or knick-knacks in every nook and cranny. Not that anything is wrong with that, especially in a college town, but in this case, it was really overkill and left little space for a guest to set down any of their belongings.

Once we completed the tour, I gave my synopsis of the interior design and asked what their feelings were. They basically said that I had reinforced what they thought about everything and that I completely validated what they were feeling.

Coincidentally, critiquing their VRBO got my juices flowing and made me start thinking about how to use my talents to help more people. I realized that with my interior design experience, designing hotels and model homes, I could guide STR hosts with the design of their properties. And so my new business, Strategic Pro Staging, Inc., was formed.

Despite all of the car craziness for the first few days of this holiday, once everything was resolved, we enjoyed a wonderful and relaxing Thanksgiving together as a family. And fortunately, they returned that rental car without the battery dying on them.

VRBOHHHHHH NOOOOOO

So here's the big question—how did my sister and her spouse end up reviewing this property, and did they get reimbursed any of their unforeseen expenses?

REVIEW: 3 out of 5 stars

They gave a 3 out of 5-star review because of the insufficient gate code and parking fiasco.

They requested a refund for the towing bill and for the inconvenience of losing a day and a half of their vacation dealing with all of the headaches.

Fortunately, the owner agreed to refund them half of their stay, which would cover the out-of-pocket expenses, and she fell all over herself with apologies.

Then, as one week turned into two weeks, and then into three weeks, and they still had not received a refund, they started thinking that the host had reneged on her offer and that it would be a loss.

But one full month later, they received a check for the agreed-upon amount. So, all was good, but it never should've happened in the first place.

Remember, your goal as a host is to have happy guests who want to return, write rave reviews, and refer you to their friends. So, let's get to it and review how this host could improve in order to receive consistent 5-star reviews.

KEY TAKEAWAYS AND DESIGN HOT TIPS

1. Make sure to make instructions extremely clear. Guests do not know everything about your property. What may be clear to you, because you live there day to day, will not be clear to your guest.
2. Design with comfort in mind. Add soft textures to hard surfaces to avoid an echo.

3. Provide guests with an array of different types of bed pillows—soft, firm, flat, and puffy.
4. Throw pillows have their place. Refrain from overdoing it.
5. Same with sports memorabilia and kitschy wall plaques with sayings. Some of these things may turn guests off. The more neutral with décor and artwork, the better.

THE 5-STAR HOST'R WAY—COMMUNICATION

As seen from this story, what may be obvious to you will not always be obvious to your guests.

When it comes to the 5-Star Host'r Way, *communication* is key.

Communication with clear instructions throughout the entire process produces happy guests who will provide you with 5-star reviews.

What's more, clear communication will prevent headaches for you—from late-night phone calls to annoyances with neighbors or other guests onsite.

Here are five key areas where communication is vital with your guests.

1. Pre-arrival and Check-in Instructions

Your guest's experience at your property begins long before their arrival. By creating clear instructions prior to their arrival, and a seamless check-in process, you will be setting the tone for their entire stay.

Make sure that your pre-arrival instructions are extremely clear. Think through every step of the arrival process for your guest.

Provide detailed check-in instructions ahead of time. Guests should have all the information they need about their upcoming check-in before leaving home.

Airbnb states, "Transparency is important for guests. Pass on information ahead of time about things that could impact a stay, like nearby construction. Do what you can to anticipate common issues, and act quickly to resolve any that arise. Being mindful of factors that are always in flux—seasons, weather, holidays, events, etc.—can help you offer solutions ahead of time."

Here are some things to include in the check-in instructions for 5-star communication:

1. Check-in time
2. The address of your property
3. Directions to the property
4. How to find the correct entrance—and the correct rental in the case of apartment buildings or other large properties with multiple accommodations
5. Explain the exact steps that guests need to take to gain access to your property—don't forget to include that "*" at the end of the gate code
6. Parking instructions—be clear on where to park and tell your guests if a specific spot is assigned to them
7. If you will be using a lockbox to store a key, give detailed instructions on where the lockbox is located and how to open it and provide the code
8. If your entrance has a keyless entry, provide the code and instructions on how to use the lock
9. The Wi-Fi details—network name and password—should be provided ahead of time as well as notated in the STR in a noticeable location
10. Provide your contact information, including both email and a direct phone number, so that guests can reach you.

The 5-Star Host

Consider adding photos of the different steps when applicable to illustrate the check-in process more precisely. Make sure each photo is clear and self-explanatory. If necessary, add text to the photos or consider taking a short video to avoid any confusion.

Create an automated template with your check-in instructions. This way, you can send the same instructions, with an exception to the entry code if that changes per guest, to every guest that books with you and improve overall guest communication.

Sample Check-in Instructions Template:

Hi [guest name],

We're excited about your upcoming stay with us at [property name], and I hope that you are looking forward to it as well!

Please remember that check-in is at [time]. The property will be ready for your arrival any time after that.

Here's all the information you will need for checking in:
Property name: [property name]
Address: [full address of property]
Parking: [provide any details]
Lockbox code: [code]

The lockbox is located at [locale] near [x]. Enter the code, and the top will open for you to collect the house keys.
Wi-Fi password: [Wi-Fi password]

If you haven't done so already, please read through our **House Manual**. *It contains everything you need to know about your upcoming stay, as* *well as recommendations for restaurants, shopping, and fun things to do in the area.*

After you have settled in, please let us know if we can do anything to make your stay more enjoyable. We're only a call or text away.

Thanks!
[Your name]

A guest who reads your check-in instructions thoroughly should be able to find, operate, and enjoy every last aspect of your property.

2. Follow Up After Check-in

A great way to communicate with your guests after their arrival is by sending a follow-up note.

The point of the follow-up is to find out if their check-in went smoothly and if they have any questions or need anything. The comfort of your guests is your number one priority, but you also want to let them know that you are striving for a 5-star review.

Sample Follow-up Template:

Good evening [Guest Name],

Thanks so much for booking my place. I hope you have settled in and are enjoying your stay. Please let me know if there is anything you need or if I can assist you in any way.

I strive for 5-star reviews, so if anything comes up that is not up to your standards, no matter how small that may be, please reach out and give me a chance to make things right. I want your stay to be an enjoyable one.

Best,

[Your Name]

3. Check Inquiries Regularly and Respond Immediately

A timely and efficient response gives the guest confidence that the STR experience will follow suit. Communicating with guests plays a significant role in whether you gain a 5-star review or not. Make sure to never ignore problems. You want to jump right on it and offer a solution.

Guests appreciate proactive and swift communication. Responding promptly lets your guests know that you care. Whereas, delaying a response gives the impression that they aren't important, and this will lead to bad reviews.

Resolve problems quickly if something comes up and keep communication open with guests. Regardless of how or when the damage occurred, you should take action to fix broken appliances or amenities. Offer assistance if your guests encounter issues, such as a tricky lock or clogged sink.

Here's the best way to handle complaints:

- Listen to what they have to say
- Don't make excuses
- Apologize for the inconvenience
- Consider a financial gesture, even a small one
- Act on the complaint immediately

Being able to resolve the issues presented in negative guest reviews can end up having a positive effect on potential guests in the end because it shows you care about them. However, leaving them unanswered will only hurt your reputation and your relationship with your future guests.

Your goal must be to reply to 100 percent of your inquiries and complaints within eight hours, but sooner is better.

4. Check-out Instructions

VRBOHHHHHH NOOOOOO

You want your guests to have a seamless experience from start to finish; therefore, your check-out process should be as explicit and smooth as your check-in process.

Winning 5-star reviews requires attention to detail.

With exceptional check-out instructions, you have the power to accomplish several things:

- Provide a friendly farewell

  Your check-out instructions are one of the ways you'll be saying goodbye to your guests and has the potential to leave a lasting impression that lingers in their minds long after they have left your home.

- Let guests know what they need to do

  Guests generally do not know what is expected of them when they leave because every host has different check-out policies. Clear check-out instructions will give guests a better idea of what needs to be done before they depart to ensure the property is in order and ensures that your property remains secure and locked between stays.

- Promote positive reviews

  An efficient check-out experience could prompt guests to leave positive reviews after their stay. When it comes to hosting, you want to take advantage of every opportunity to impress your guests, and the check-out instructions are just another opportunity to do that.

Your check-out instructions should include:

- Check-out time
- Cleanup instructions
- How to lock up and what to do with keys
- Final goodbye

Sample Check-out Instructions Template:

Dear [Guest Name],

As the end of your stay is approaching, we wanted to say thank you for choosing our property for your getaway. We hope your time here has been enjoyable!

Here is some key information that you'll need for your departure:

A friendly reminder that check-out is between [time] and [time].

No need to worry about cleaning up; we'll do that for you. However, we would greatly appreciate it if you could strip the bed of used linens and move the trash bin outside the property when you leave.

Before you leave, don't forget to double-check that you have all your belongings!

Then, we kindly ask you to switch off the air conditioning and the lights in each room.

We also ask that you make sure all the windows are closed and that you don't forget to lock the back and front doors. You can once again leave your keys [in the lock box/provide the code].

It was truly a pleasure hosting you. If you have any feedback for us, we would love it if you could leave a review on [travel portal]. Every review means the world to us!

Lastly, have a safe trip home. We hope to see you again very soon!

Best,

[Your Name]

5. Ask for Reviews

Make sure to ask every person who stayed to review your property. Customer reviews make all the difference.

Listings with 5-star reviews increase your odds of appearing at top of searches and increase your traffic because people often pick the most highly rated places that many previous customers review.

Research published by Fan & Fuel notes that consumers not only want to see reviews on positive aspects, but they also look for all the graphic details of any problems people have had, how you've responded to complaints, and so on. They cite that:

- 47% spread the word about a positive experience
- 95% shout from the rooftops about a negative experience
- 92% of consumers hesitate to make a purchase when there are no customer reviews

Tip: Don't have any history yet? Let a few friends and family who have stayed there review the properties, leaving honest, accurate, and positive feedback.

Sample Request for Review Template:

Hi [Guest Name],

Hope you had a ton of fun on your trip.

Thanks so much for being so respectful of our place during your stay, and thanks for keeping the house so nice and tidy! It is greatly appreciated!

If you don't mind, I would love to ask you for a huge favor. Reviews and ratings have a significant impact on hosts as well as guests. I was hoping I could ask you to leave me a 5-star review if you feel I deserved it. I work very hard for 5-star reviews, and I would appreciate it very much if you left me feedback about how I am doing.

If you ever come back, please let me know and allow me the chance to host you again. If you ever have a suggestion on how to improve, please message me privately. I would love to discuss your feedback in detail. I am constantly working to improve the experience for all of my guests.

Thanks so much,

[Your Name]

After encouraging your guests to leave a review, ensure you do the same for them.

5-STAR HOST'R ACTION PLAN

1. Follow the design hot tips
2. Design your check-in template for your property
3. Design your follow-up instructions template
4. Design your check-out template
5. Design your request for reviews template

Chapter 3

AIR B & Beware

It was our third wedding anniversary, and my loving, generous husband wanted to surprise me with a trip to a place I had never been before.

He had lived in Tampa, Florida, in the past and was a big fan of Florida and knew that I was not. He wanted to change my mind.

So, he whisked me away on a trip to the world-famous beach at Siesta Key. If you have never been, I highly recommend it. The sand feels like powdered sugar between your toes, and it does not get hot. It is unlike any other beach in the entire world.

As with any trip my husband plans, he researched places to stay extensively. He found a cute half of a duplex with one bedroom within walking distance to the beach.

This Airbnb was unlike many others in the area because it provided access to a "private beach." Nothing could be better, right?

Unfortunately, we were about to find out that this was not always true!

As soon as we arrived, the host was there to greet us. My husband had not realized we were renting the property that she used as her home. She was just leaving for the week. This made her a bit more sensitive to how we would treat her property.

Off to a bad start. She had not advertised in any way that this rental was her home. Due to our past experiences with this type of situation, we would never have booked this place. Oh well, we were in paradise, so we shrugged it off.

The host told us she was going to take us on a tour. First, she showed us the living areas and then she showed us the bedroom and bathroom. There was one other room with a closed door that she asked us to go not into.

This was all fine and good, but then she said she wanted to take us on a tour of the beach. So, we tagged along behind her as she took us down the boardwalk to the beautiful powder-soft white sandy beach. We could've found this on our own, but she claims she wanted to see our faces when we first saw the beach.

Honestly, it looked gorgeous, but I did not want to walk in the sand with my winter clothes, socks, and shoes on. I preferred to be in beach attire when stepping in the sand, but she insisted. So, we took off our shoes and socks and rolled up our pant legs.

My husband was right on the money. This was the softest sand I had ever walked in, and it truly felt like powdered sugar. It was the most amazing thing ever.

We were anxious to get our vacation started, but that was not her plan. She proceeded to give us a laundry list of chores to perform for her and to chat with us about trivial things for about twenty to thirty more minutes. It was as if she was interviewing us to make sure she could trust us in her home.

Once we returned to her property, she went through another laundry list of chores she wanted us to take care of for her during the week that she would not be there. This was a bit annoying, I must say, but I held my tongue.

Finally, after what felt like the longest hour of my life, she left us alone, and we began our vacation. She told us she would not bother us during our stay but to contact her if we needed anything.

Ahhhhh, what a relief! "Let's get this vacation started," I declared!

We couldn't wait to get unpacked, put our swimsuits on, and run to the beach. But here's where the problems began…

Since she lived there and the square footage was sparse, we found nowhere to put our clothes. The closet was jampacked full of her clothing, as were the dresser drawers. And there was barely any room around the bed to place our suitcases on the ground.

Then, we found that the same held true for the bathroom. There was literally no counter space for anything, nor was there space in the shower to put our shampoo and soap.

But we were at the beach and wanted to make the best of it. So, we put on our swimsuits and headed out for a glorious day in the sun.

We made a quick trip to the store to grab a few things for our breakfast throughout the week. When we went to put our items in the refrigerator, we realized there was no room for our food. Her refrigerator was even jampacked full of her stuff.

I mean, what was this woman thinking? Where did she expect us to put our belongings?

I had to keep telling myself, *calm down; you're at the beach.*

The following morning, we received a phone call from the host asking if we had watered her plants. One of the chores she had assigned to us was to water her outdoor plants daily. Again, I found this a bit annoying. But I followed her request.

Mid-morning, we loaded up the wagon with beach chairs, an umbrella and towels that she had left us. This was definitely a perk when booking, as we did not want to purchase these items that we would not be able to take back home with us.

We located the perfect spot at the private beach and set up our chairs and towels. But we soon realized that the canvas was ripped at the seat of one of the chairs, so you basically fell through, and the frame was broken on the other one, so it tipped over. It was obvious that we were not the cause of this, and the guests before us had broken them.

But wouldn't you think the host—or cleaning crew—would make sure the beach chairs were in a functioning condition before each new stay? Especially when advertising this as one of your extra amenities to entice beach-seeking vacationers. Most hosts would know to replace their beach equipment annually to avoid heavy wear and tear and possible accidents. I guess not this host!

Fortunately, we had the mindset to make the best of it. After all, we were on the nicest beach in the USA! So, we put the chairs aside and laid our towels right on the beach. We were not going to let these mishaps get the best of us.

After an hour or so, we felt our skin getting burned, so we decided to put up the umbrella. I'm guessing you figured this out already. Yup… it was broken also. Aye yai yaiiii!!!

Stay calm, stay calm, stay calm, I repeated to myself.

Now we reached day three. As one might expect, we ran out of the roll of toilet paper that she had left us. We were not in the position to be able to go to a store to buy some, so we did what any guest would do. We started searching the house for more toilet paper.

When we came up empty, I decided to take an uncertain act—I decided to go into that bedroom she told us to avoid in hopes that I would find some extra rolls.

I was surprised to find the door was not even locked. I turned the handle, and what I saw before me was piles of junk. Lots and lots of boxes and junk. But would you believe that on top of all that junk was an unopened 12-pack of toilet paper rolls?

So, we helped ourselves to a new roll of toilet paper. I mean, what kind of host does not leave extra toilet paper for their guests? This was starting to become a pattern. I was baffled at how this woman could have become an Airbnb Superhost!

On to day four—trash day. Another one of our assigned chores was to take out the trash. We had barely collected any trash but wouldn't you know, she had left several large bags and trash cans full of her own trash for us to dispose of.

Normally, this wouldn't have been a big deal, but her home was set way back, so we had to walk nearly half a block to place all of her personal trash by the curb to be picked up. Then, at the end of the day, we had to bring all the cans back to her home.

Of course, this meant she called us again to ensure we handled her chores properly.

Come on, I thought—*we're supposed to be on vacation, and you said you would leave us alone.*

Now we're at day five. *At last, one day to ourselves,* so we thought. This host had the gall to call us yet again! This time, we did not answer her call as we really did not want to be bothered.

Her voicemail simply said, "Just checking in with you to make sure everything's going okay."

What?! Why???

Needless to say, we did not return this call because we had just spoken with her the day before, and everything was going fine. We had no need to speak with her again.

Next up, day six—yup, of course, you guessed it!

She called again! This time, she wanted to repeat the check-out chores she had already covered with us on day one.

Did she think we had poor memories? I was beyond irritated at this point.

I don't know about you, but her list of check-out chores seemed far too extensive for a paying guest to complete, especially when we had paid her an additional cleaning fee.

What's your opinion?

Here's her list of our check-out chores:
1. Wash all dishes and put them away, including all those in the dishwasher—which meant planning ahead to make sure the load was completed before our departure and to leave enough time to do this.
2. Wipe down all the kitchen and bathroom counters.

3. Tie up all bags of trash and put them in the trash cans beside the house. Put new trash bags in all the interior trash cans.

4. Ensure the beach towels are washed, folded, and put back in the linen closet—again, this needed to be planned in advance so this load was dry before we left.

5. Remove all the sheets and bath towels, put them in the washing machine, add soap and start the washing machine.

This is too much! Am I right?

Here comes day seven—the work begins. Cleaning and more cleaning, and that's on top of the packing we had to do.

We were told to be out by 10:00 am, yet the cleaning people came knocking on the door at 9:30 am.

What exactly was left for this cleaning person to do? We had done everything except for re-making the bed.

At this point, we could not wait to get out of there. What a damper this woman had put on our vacation. Who on earth requests their guests to do all of their daily chores for them while they are gone? This was completely out of hand!

I'm betting you think our story ends here, correct? But it didn't.

As you know, Airbnb allows both the host and the guest to review each other.

We loved the location, so we wanted to give it 5-stars, but come on. I mean, seriously. She advertised her place incorrectly, and we had nowhere to put our belongings for the entire week. Her beach equipment was broken. The number of chores she had us complete was over the top. And she called us nearly every day to check on us.

Therefore, we gave her 3-stars, which I believed was far too high for the burdens she put upon our vacation. But we were trying to be nice. Boy, that was a mistake!

Almost immediately after we posted our 3-star review, we got a message that she had reviewed us.

We were expecting 5-stars because we completed *all* her daily chores as requested, and we actually left her place cleaner than when we arrived.

We opened our laptop to find that this crazy woman only gave us 3-stars.

Her remarks were as follows, "I would have given you 5-stars, but you did not return my calls."

Are you kidding me? We spoke to her every day of our vacation except for one day. What was this lady smoking?

Who wants to talk to the host every single day when you're on vacation? We certainly don't.

This definitely makes you consider the review process and the flaws in the system. It is basically tit for tat. We did not get a fair review, and we gave her a higher rating than she should've received.

Ironically, we have been back to Siesta Key four times since that vacation. But each time, we have chosen to stay elsewhere—even though other places cost us more and did not have access to the private beach.

The truth is, you couldn't pay us to return to her place.

What a shame that is! Most hosts would be thrilled to have repeat guests that they know they can trust.

But alas, it was her loss.

REVIEW: 3 out of 5 stars, and that was considerably too high

So out of curiosity, after we returned home, I polled several of my friends and family members to see what they thought of our experience. I wanted to make sure that the "general public" had the same expectations about staying in an Airbnb as we did. Here is one of my conversations—which coincidentally matched the responses of whom I polled:

Me: How do you feel about somebody saying, "You need to put the sheets and towels in the washing machine and start it before you leave?"

Interviewee 1: NO! That is not my duty; I'm paying for cleaning. Right?!

Me: Okay. How do you feel about having someone say, "You need to water my plants while I'm gone?"

Interviewee 2: No!

Interviewee 1: I should not have to do all this. I should not have a job.

Interviewee 2: Wow! "You need to water my plants?!" This lady sounds ridiculous.

Me: And when we first got there, she took us on a lengthy tour, and we just wanted to start our vacation. I wanted to scream, "Could you just stop, please? Let us be!" Then she said she'd leave us alone, and she called almost every day.

Interviewee 1: NO!! We're on vacation. We're not here to talk to you every day!

How would *you* answer those questions? How are you running your own STR business? Are you expecting your guests to complete a laundry list of chores—no pun intended—and most cleaning before their departure?

If so, you may want to rethink some of your guest procedures, as most vacationers simply want to relax and get away from the daily drudge.

Note: Coincidentally, Airbnb must have had a lot of complaints regarding this because they added a policy in late 2022 addressing hidden cleaning fees and checkout tasks. In fact, Brian Chesky, Airbnb co-founder & CEO states, "I've heard you loud and clear—you feel like prices aren't transparent and checkout tasks are a pain. You shouldn't have to do unreasonable checkout tasks, such as stripping the beds, doing the laundry, or vacuuming."

Thank goodness AirBnB is taking action on this moving forward. But if you list your STR on other OTAs or your own direct booking site, please keep this mind. Nobody likes doing all those chores when they're trying to pack up and leave.

KEY TAKEAWAYS AND DESIGN HOT TIPS

1. Remove your own belongings from closets, drawers, cabinets, shelves, and the refrigerator. Guests do not like the feeling that they are intruding on your space and are not welcome there.

2. Provide luggage racks, especially if closet space is limited, so guests do not have to bend down to the floor to grab items from their suitcases.

3. Don't visit or contact guests needlessly. Be aware of their personal boundaries. Engage with them when it's welcomed. Give them privacy and make it clear you're available if they need you.

4. Let guests know that you trust them to treat your place as their own.

5. Do not expect your guests to water indoor or outdoor plants for you; they are your guest.

6. Respect personal preferences and adjust things to each person's needs. For example, remove nuts, or

perfumed items for guests who mention an allergy or sensitivities.

7. While it is not the guest's responsibility to clean the whole house, it is not unreasonable to ask them to tidy up a little before they leave your STR rental property.

   Asking them to do tasks like taking the trash to the trash bin outside your house or washing dishes is not asking too much. However, if an STR host charges a cleaning fee, they should not expect guests to do too much.

8. If you would like your guests to strip the bed of linens and sheets and gather the used towels, the most important thing to remember is to give them clear directions on what to do with them.

   Many hosts ask their guests to either leave these in a pile on the floor or throw them in a laundry basket. Do not expect them to start the laundry for you, especially if they pay a cleaning fee.

9. Hire a good cleaning crew and have them strip the beds and start the laundry.

10. Do not give your guests a bad review simply to spite them for not giving you a 5-star review. Find out why they did not give you a stellar review and fix it moving forward.

THE 5-STAR HOST'R WAY—BRANDING

Branding has always been a crucial part of business, and it's more important now than ever before.

The STR market today is intensely competitive, and the competition is only increasing, so you need to step up your game to ensure you stand out in a crowded space. The best way to do this is by creating a strong brand that will attract people's attention. Cohesive branding changes the way people perceive your property, and you become memorable. You definitely don't want to overlook this step.

In its most basic form, branding is a way of distinguishing yourself from your competition, and it clarifies what you offer that makes you the better choice. If done correctly, branding will drive traffic and help you to stand out from your competition.

Have you ever wondered how we found hotels before the Internet? I know, I know—some of you weren't even born yet, but humor me…

It was as simple as remembering the special hotel brands and slogans from the commercials we saw on TV or from the logos we saw as we drove by them.

Some were known for their price point, be it high or low. For example:

> Motel 6: Their brand was known for charging guests the very low price of $6 a night. The hotel's name reflected this as well as the recognizable "6" as their logo. Their ads repeated the slogan, "We'll leave the light on for you." Now, who could forget that?

Some were known for a specific type of travelers, such as families, adventurers, or executives. For example:

> Days Inn: The brand's mission is simple: "We make hotel travel possible for all." Their goal is to provide "The Best Value Under the Sun," as depicted by the company's logo of the sun. This chain has many properties located near outdoor attractions because they target outdoors enthusiasts and adventure seekers.

Some were known for the amenities they offered. For example:

> The DoubleTree: The Double Tree is best known for its famous complimentary warm chocolate chip cookies.

And some were known for their location, often right off the highways or near an airport. For example:

> La Quinta Inn: These hotels are often located in suburban areas and near airports. Their cheerful slogan says, "Wake up on the bright side."

Hotels knew the importance of pinpointing their ideal guests and building a memorable brand around that.

So, what lessons can we learn from these notable hotel brands?

If you have a strong brand for your property, people will be more likely to remember it. A property without branding isn't going to stay in a potential guest's mind for very long. However, a property that has branding will be much more memorable.

Branding encompasses the following tasks:

- Naming your property
- Describing your property
- Highlighting the incentives and experiences to offer your guests
- Designing your property
- Photographing your property
- Advertising your property

Basically, branding will affect every aspect of your STR and will make everything cohesive if you do it right.

But it can also do the opposite if done incorrectly or not at all.

So let's get started and do it the right way …

1. Name Your Property

Have you ever seen the TV show called *My Lottery Dream Home* on HGTV?

The host, David Bromstad, takes recent lottery winners on house hunts for their new dream homes. It's an opportunity most of us can only dream about—winning the lottery and then being shown around three stunning properties by a design expert.

But what really sticks out to me in this show is how creative David is in selecting a unique name for each property they view. By giving each property a name, they retain the uniqueness of each home; subsequently, the lottery winners can remember the property they like by name.

For instance, in Cape Cod, Massachusetts, they saw the following three homes:

- The Sandpiper
- Gooseberry Grove
- Gull Cottage

And here are some fun ones from Orlando, Florida:

- Magnolia Lane
- The Pink Palm Hideaway
- Mockingbird Manor

But my favorites were from another show, *Beachfront Bargain Hunt*, set in the Florida Keys:

- Between Two Palms
- Holy Mackerel
- Slow M'Ocean

Now those are memorable, right?

In its most basic form, you want to give your STR a name based on its location or property type.

From there, move on and get creative. Think of something catchy and memorable that will attract your TIG.

2. Brand with Social Media Marketing

The cool thing about naming your STR is that you can then use it as a handle for a variety of marketing purposes:

1. Instagram: @gooseberrygrove

    Then you can follow hashtags on Instagram and get notified when someone posts about you.

2. Facebook: Create a business page and brand your domain with your property name, so it becomes Facebook.com/gooseberrygrove

3. You can even create a custom URL on Airbnb, for example: www.airbnb.com/h/gooseberrygrove
4. Buy a domain name that matches the name of your property, www.gooseberrygrove.com, and direct that to your direct booking website—more on this in Chapter 7.

Do you see how just this small amount of branding makes your property more memorable to potential guests?

3. Create Your Title

Whether you are listing your STR on OTAs or on your own direct booking website, it is vital to develop a strong title.

Most sites allow fifty characters for the title. However, you'll want to put your strongest keywords at the beginning of the title because only a few of the words are seen in the thumbnail version.

To come up with your title, think about communicating a selling point or a special amenity you offer.

- Example: 1 Block from Beach

The goal is to sell the space. Draw potential guests in so they can picture themselves staying there.

- Why is the kitchen easy to cook in?
- Why is the bed so comfy?
- Why is the shower so good?

The more descriptive you are, the better.

It's not a good idea to state the number of bedrooms and bathrooms in your title because guests have already narrowed their search for this, and you don't want to waste precious characters on something they already know.

Bad title: 2 BR/1 Bath Elegant Home in Downtown District

Good title: Rooftop Patio with Views & Hot Tub, Plus Parking

Try to think outside the box and get as creative as you can in order to stand out from the competition.

Your title can always be changed, so just start with something and test it out. After all, done is better than perfect.

4. Write Your Property Description

The description is where you should address aspects relevant to your property and its location. This might be the only thing a potential guest reads.

Define your guests' optimal emotional experience—what do you want guests to feel when interacting with you and staying at your place?

Always be accurate with your listing information. This will impact your guests' stay. For them, it's critical that you're honest and accurate about what you're offering.

Provide information only if it's useful to your TIG.

Market your property's best features, but also be realistic about what they will get. Ensure that you do not over-promise and then not deliver. You do not want disappointed guests.

Communicate both positive and negative aspects of your listing by setting expectations before the guest checks in. You don't want your guests to be caught off guard by anything, so be completely transparent.

Be brutally honest about the three things that most people like about your listing and the two things they do not like. The more authentic you are in your listing description, the more trust you are building.

When people trust you, it takes away the worry about them booking and not being sure if this is the right place or not.

Let them decide what they are or aren't willing to put up with, but don't surprise them.

When guests arrive at your STR, they expect to get exactly what you promised online. It would be even better if you over-deliver. Don't paint too rosy a picture, or your guests could be disappointed.

Make your description easier to read by adding bullet points.

Also, it is helpful to add a call-to-action to your description—for example, Book Now—to maximize your conversion rates.

Lastly, be sure that your listing details are kept up to date and are complete.

5. Build a Brand Package and Styling Guide

We've discussed the importance of approaching your STR like a business, even if you only have one listing. Part of what business owners do to solidify their brand is to create a styling guide for marketing purposes.

Your brand package should be cohesive as well as aesthetically pleasing so that it meshes well together. A strong brand voice makes you stand out and will help you reach your TIG.

Create a styling guide for your STR business that includes the following:

- Color palette: Select three to five harmonious colors that match the vibe of your space—colors help a website stand out; be vibrant
- Font styles: Select two to three fonts to use consistently through all of your advertising
- Design a logo: This can be a business name if you have multiple STRs, or it could be a logo of your property name, if you only plan on having one STR
- Bio: Write a paragraph or two about yourself and why you decided to become a host
- Imagery: Include photos of the property and of you for your bio
- Name, title, and description of the property: Covered in previous steps of this lesson
- Mission statement: What do you want your TIG's optimal emotional experience to be

- Optional: Produce a promo video that you can post on social media or send to press outlets showing what guests can expect during their stay—tell a story in two to three minutes

Once you have this in place, consider designing stationery with your logo for guests to use while at your property—as hotels do—or provide pre-stamped postcards with a photo of the space for guests to mail easily.

Similar to hotels, by creating a brand, you become memorable. A potential guest may not be ready to book just yet, but they probably won't forget it after seeing it for only a moment, simply because of your brand. It sticks out from others, and eventually, when they're ready to book, they'll return to your listing.

It's time to get your property out there and build brand awareness. OTA's are not going to do that for you.

5-STAR HOST'R ACTION PLAN

1. Clean out space in closets, drawers, cabinets, cupboards, and the refrigerator, so there is space for your guest's belongings.
2. Research good cleaning crews.
3. Have your cleaning crew check all furniture and amenities to make sure they are in good working order. Replace what is broken prior to your next guest's arrival.
4. Brainstorm a memorable name for your property and set up your social media with the property name, as directed in Step 2.
5. Come up with a catchy title for your STR.
6. Write an accurate description for your STR and entice your TIG through emotions.
7. Put together a styling package.

Chapter 4

INSTRUCTION OVERLOAD

It was that time of year again. The crisp fall air had settled in, and it was once again time to gather at my father's house for Thanksgiving. Similar to years past, my oldest sister and her spouse began searching for a nearby Airbnb to stay in for the week.

They knew they did not want to stay in the same place as the previous year, with the car fiasco, so they chose what appeared to be a much better fit for them.

Boy, were they wrong!

At least their flight was on time, and their check engine light didn't pop on in their rental car.

But as soon as they arrived at the property, it was impossible to get in the front door. The owners left a key hidden in a lockbox on the front door handle, but once my sister retrieved it, the key would not open the door. She wiggled and wiggled it and tried it in different positions, but nothing worked.

Eventually, they noticed a note on the door with instructions on how to maneuver the key, but the message didn't make any sense. They tried ceaselessly for over thirty minutes to get that door to open with no luck. They had been traveling all day and were utterly exhausted. Besides, they had plans to meet friends for dinner that night and did not want to be late.

Finally, they reached the owner by phone and told him they could not get into the property. He said, "Well, didn't you read the note?"

Oh dear, they're thinking, *this is getting off to a great start.*

But they knew they were running out of time to meet their friends, so they left without being able to get inside the house. And that is not what you want after a long journey. Right? You want to be able to get in and unload your baggage and freshen up.

Nonetheless, the owner came over while they were at dinner and fixed the lock so they could get in once they returned from dinner.

But once they were inside, the air temperature felt freezing. Obviously, the thermostat was on, but it wasn't as warm as they wanted it. So, they went to the thermostat in the hallway and found a bunch of sticky notes above it. It was one of those programmable Nest units. But it was so complicated that even when trying to follow the posted instructions, they could not figure it out for the life of them.

So, they called the owner again and asked him, "How do you get this thing to work?"

And again, he replied, "Didn't you read the instructions?"

They replied, "Yes, but it didn't make any sense."

So, once he walked them through it and they got it to work, they were astonished to hear how loud it was. *Surely something is wrong because nobody's furnace is this loud,* they thought. They said it felt like a jet taking off.

Once again, they called the owner to make sure they didn't need a mechanic to come in and fix it. But he told them, "That's just the way it sounds. Once it hits its target heat, it will turn off." And it did. But this was a very open floor plan, and the furnace was off the kitchen behind a door, so you could hear the whole thing just rumbling.

Unfortunately, this made it hard to go to sleep and stay asleep if it started up again in the middle of the night. It also made it difficult to read. Here's their recollection.

INSTRUCTION OVERLOAD

"The living room was not user-friendly at all. This place was marketed as an open floorplan in retro style. And when we went in, all it looked like was Goodwill furniture. I mean, the fabric on the chairs was torn, where your arms lay. And what I didn't like about it was the large cathedral ceiling with very bad lighting. So, this goes into my wanting to read at night. I could not find a comfortable chair or a chair with enough light to relax and read. Once I found a place to sit down, then the furnace would kick on. It would scare the shit out of me. I'd jump a foot because it was so loud. And finally, it was warm, but I was always sitting there uncomfortable, on this hard thing, covered with a couple of blankets, waiting for it to go on. And then, when it finally did go on, it echoed. It was just an unfriendly, uninviting living room."

There were so many bad things about this house. But the problem with the living room was not the worst of it. This property was a two-story home, and the owners must've had babies because baby gates were everywhere, including at the top and bottom of the stairs.

Now, I don't know if you've tried to unlock a baby gate before, but they're really hard to figure out, especially if you have luggage. In my sister's case, she finally figured out how to open it up, grabbed her bags, took them up the stairs and found another locked gate at the top of the stairs. Imagine figuring out where you will put your luggage while opening the baby gate while standing in this very small area without falling down the stairs. Right?

Next, imagine it's in the middle of the night, and you wake up because it is too hot. You go downstairs to adjust the thermostat, and you're greeted by this crazy baby gate. It's dark, so you bring a flashlight, but you have to figure out how to open the gate at the top of the stairs and then fumble with the one at the bottom of the stairs.

Of course, they automatically shut behind you, so once you've adjusted the thermostat, you have to repeat the process once again when you go back up the stairs to bed. My sister and her spouse constantly feared falling down the stairs.

At this point, you're probably wondering why they didn't just remove the gates or leave them open, right? Well, they were permanently screwed into the wall, so you could not remove them. Nor could you leave them ajar because you couldn't open the adjacent door at the bottom of the stairs if the gate was left open and the one at the top opened into the hallway, so you couldn't walk around if you left that one open. Therefore, that one had to remain closed as well.

But unfortunately, the difficulties of this house do not stop there.

The owners had recently remodeled the kitchen and were very proud of it. But unfortunately, this meant that they were overly cautious of any damage occurring, so they had these little signs all over the place like, "Don't put anything hot on the surface, or it'll ruin it." And, "This is how you use the sink." There were fourteen little signs in the kitchen alone, explaining everything.

In addition, they had remodeled the upstairs bathroom, so little signs were posted all over that room as well. But after reading all those notes, in addition to the House Manual, they still couldn't figure out how to turn on the shower in the bathroom, so they had to take baths for their entire stay. They knew that if they called the owner again, he would say what he always said, "Didn't you read the manual?"

Apparently, these particular owners loved new gadgets. But unless you live there and you know how to use them, they don't make sense to outsiders. They're all very complicated with a steep learning curve that requires all these signs to explain how to use them, which is not appealing to an STR guest.

My sister mentioned that the House Manual had no paragraph indentations, so it was next to impossible to read or understand. Yet the owner expected his guests to study it and follow what it said. But it was ten times the size that most House Manuals are, and he wanted them to read through this entire thing?

Nobody wants that when they are on vacation. They want a simple place.

INSTRUCTION OVERLOAD

In fact, my sister told me that she always read the manuals when she went somewhere new, but that this one was unreadable. It was like a book he had written and he was super proud of it—"Go look in the manual." Yeah.

She told me that she actually read it aloud one night for some humor. He used as many big words as he could to describe things; it was not concise. She said, "You could sort of see why he was doing it, because the place was very complicated, which is not a good thing for an Airbnb."

So, this is when they realized—and I tend to agree with them—that they hated renting a place that was someone's full-time residence, even if they shoved their stuff out of the way.

For instance, in the kitchen was a pot with some ghastly-looking thing soaking in it. It's as if the owners rushed out for the weekend and left everything on the counter.

Not to mention the bedrooms—the jam-packed closets left no space to put luggage or clothes.

Here's how they described it:

"The first bedroom was in an office with a bed in it. The bed was placed against the wall as you walked in the door. Opposite the bed was a portable wardrobe, like clothes on a roller, and behind that was a packed closet and a whole bunch of boxes piled up. Off to the side were a desk with a computer, stacks of books, and piles of paper on it. And then they had this baby fencing all around that area. So you couldn't go in that. There was literally no space to put anything. I had to cram my suitcase over by the bed."

Additionally, the TV was also in this room, and it was the only TV in the whole house. Imagine trying to relax in this messy-looking room, complete with this cage thing, and then you realize that you have to use a very complex remote control to get anything on the television.

The second bedroom was no better. It held a bassinet or Pack 'N Play crammed to the brim with baby stuff. Then, off to the side were boxes filled with more baby stuff. There was a large dresser, but every one of the drawers was over full of underwear, socks, and all of their stuff. There was simply no space to put your own belongings anywhere. The only option was to live out of your suitcase. But finding a spot for that was difficult, not to mention unappealing, because the floor was covered with disgusting old shag carpet.

Which brings us to the design of this property.

They advertised this home as "retro design," but they had no idea what they were doing. It appeared they had simply gone to Goodwill, gotten some old chairs from the fifties or the sixties, and claimed it was retro.

The problem with the chairs they selected is they were very rigid. Once again, they had not considered comfort for their guests—which is interesting because they lived there. One could only assume they figured the chairs were cool-looking and kind of go together because they're kind of the same era.

In the living room was a couch and weird chair under a swinging wicker light. Apparently, this was supposed to be the reading chair, but the light did not produce enough wattage for reading.

Moreover, the setup was not great for conversation. It obviously wasn't a TV area. The light wasn't good enough for reading. The chairs weren't comfortable enough for sitting. So, why go into the living room?

Sadly, there wasn't much thought or consideration put into why guests would you use that space, and it was the biggest space in the house—over a third of the square footage.

If you can believe it, after hearing all the negatives about this place, my sister told me about one good thing. The picnic table off the kitchen was comfortable.

"What? A picnic table? Those are usually so uncomfortable," I remarked.

My sister told me she would take a throw pillow from the sofa to make it softer to sit on but that it was the only spot where the light was good enough to read. It also looked out onto a very nice

INSTRUCTION OVERLOAD

patio. But since it was the middle of winter, they didn't ever go on the patio.

She said she spent a lot of time working on her laptop and reading at that table. Plus, it was located right off the kitchen, so she could easily grab some coffee and munchies.

One final note about this property that's worth bringing up...

It was obvious that these owners were of the Christian faith because they had crosses and religious items throughout the house, and next to the bed were books about why homosexuality is bad.

I feel that your beliefs are your choice but put the religious items and those books away if you rent your place out to guests. You never know who your guests are and their beliefs; do your best not to alienate them with your personal beliefs.

REVIEW: 3 out of 5-stars

My sister and her spouse gave this property a 3 out of 5 because it was uncomfortable, there was no place to put their own belongings, and the instruction overload was out of control.

KEY TAKEAWAYS AND DESIGN HOT TIPS

The biggest takeaway from this story is that if you are planning on leaving your personal home for a brief period to rent it to guests, make sure you clear out space for them to move in. They are paying you good money for this space, and it is not right to make them feel as if they are intruding. Be sure to leave space for them to put their belongings.

Ideally, a guest should find adequate closet space and empty drawers for them to use in both the bedrooms and the bathroom. At a minimum, clear out hanging closet space and provide empty hangers for guests to hang their clothes and empty shelf space for their folded clothes.

As a last resort, provide an empty hanging wardrobe along with hangers in the bedroom, but only if there is still space to walk around comfortably.

Otherwise, why even consider renting your place out?

Always think about the guest's comfort first.

Here are a few more takeaways:

1. Ensure that the key opens the front door without having to jiggle it. Consider putting in a keyless entry mechanism.
2. Remove baby gates for your guests. They are a hazard. You can secure them back on the wall once your guests leave.
3. If you're going to have other people stay in your home, make things simple. If it's too hard to figure out to turn the furnace or the shower on, change it out to something easier. The same goes for everything throughout the house.
4. Remove your personal belongings from as many flat surfaces throughout the house as possible. Guests will have personal items that they will want to place there.
5. Nobody wants to spend their vacation reading through a huge manual of instructions or see dozens of notes posted everywhere with messages about what to do.
6. If you have items that might keep guests up at night, such as a noisy furnace, provide this information in the property listing so that a guest won't be surprised by it.
7. Ensure your furniture is comfortable and your lighting is adequate for reading. Many people work and like to read while on vacation.

8. Remove accessories and books that may offend a guest's views—religion, politics, sexual preference, etcetera. Religious or political items like crosses on the wall or pictures of the president have no place inside your STR.

9. Remove personal items like family photos which may make your guest feel as if they are invading someone else's home and space.

10. The number one cause of injury in STRs is from trips and falls. Make sure there are no areas with loose carpet or throw rugs where someone could trip.

11. Don't buy secondhand furniture; someone is probably getting rid of it for a reason. Only buy new so that you know the history of your furnishings.

THE 5-STAR HOST'R WAY—HOUSE MANUAL AND SAFETY TIPS

As the world of STRs get increasingly competitive, it becomes much more important to greet guests with genuine hospitality.

When thinking about hospitality, 5-Star Host'rs need to realize that guests are usually flooded with information about their STR stay. From check-in instructions to house rules, it's easy for them to feel overloaded before the trip even begins.

A great way to combat this feeling of overload is to provide a House Manual; some hosts refer to it as a Welcome Book.

The benefits of providing a House Manual for your guests are two-fold.

For the guest, it makes them feel welcome, and provides them with all the necessary information about their stay.

For the host, you will avoid many phone calls, including those late-night interruptions, from your aggravated guests about how to use each amenity in your house.

The House Manual is a compilation of all the information your guests will need during their stay. This can range from recommendations to house rules to check-out details.

Give your guests a digital copy of your House Manual before they arrive, but also provide a printed hardcopy at the property.

This hardcopy can be presented in different formats, such as a binder or a 3-ring notebook. Make sure to add labeled tabs for easy navigation. Realize that most guests will not read your House Manual from cover to cover. Providing sections will allow your guests to page through to a section they might want to read before the others.

Remember that your guests are likely to be unfamiliar with your property and may not have ever visited your town or city before. Hence, the key is that every section should be helpful for first-time guests in your area and home and provide guests with the tools they need to navigate their stay independently.

What to Include in Your House Manual

1. Welcome Information

Use the first section of your House Manual to welcome your guests to your STR.

Make sure to thank them for booking and wish them a wonderful stay. Let them know that you are available to answer any questions they might have and provide your contact details.

Finish off by asking them to read through the entire House Manual, as it contains important information.

2. Safety and Emergency Contact Numbers

Be aware that guests staying in your property likely don't know their surroundings. Guests are presuming your place is safe. More importantly, you are responsible for your guests' lives while they are at your property. If they know you have their safety in mind, they'll feel more at ease.

Hotels provide emergency exit signs, fire extinguishers, and exit maps. As a host, you need to manage those risks and include the following:

- Location of the circuit panel-breaker box
- Location of the main water shut off
- Location of the gas valve shut off
- Location of fire extinguishers—must have one on each level of property that is mounted on the wall
- Location of first aid kit
- Any other critical information they might need to know—for example, if poisonous snakes live in the area

Remember, guests don't have all the resources they would find in their own homes. Include the names and contact information for emergency contacts if any problems occur.

- Nearest medical clinic or hospital
- Nearest police department
- Nearest fire station
- A national emergency hotline/contact number
- The nearest vet—if your rental is pet-friendly
- Your private security company, if you use one

Tip: Include the full address of the STR property in case not all guests are aware of it.

3. Arrival and Departure Instructions

A copy of your check-in and check-out instructions should be included in your House Manual to prevent any confusion or complaints from your guests, especially about the check-out time.

Start by adding a nice note, hoping that their check-in went smoothly. Add specific parking information and any access codes, if applicable.

4. Login Instructions and Passwords

Create a separate section for all login instructions and passwords to include the guest Wi-Fi name and password and any details about the Wi-Fi, including router and Internet restrictions.

You should also include passwords for TV access, Roku, or streaming services.

5. House Rules and Property Policies

House rules allow hosts to explain what behavior is and is not allowed in their STR. All STRs have their own set of rules, so even if your guest has stayed at many other STRs, that's not to say they'll know your house rules unless you spell them out clearly.

Listing your house rules and clear instructions for guests as to what is expected of them during their stay can also prevent accidents or misunderstandings between you and your guests.

If trash is collected on a certain day of the week, you'll want to let your guests know so they don't miss the opportunity to throw out the garbage.

Use this section to remind guests how to leave your property in good condition.

- Trash day and instructions for taking out the trash
- Garbage and recycling instructions
- What to do with excess food
- Cleaning expectations of guests upon departure
- Policies on smoking in the house
- Policies on pets

INSTRUCTION OVERLOAD

- Policies on parties and extra guests and if there is a fee involved for extra guests—post the maximum number of people allowed in your property
- Mention if shoes are not allowed to be worn inside the home
- Spell out noise restrictions—for example, refrain from making noise past 11 pm
- Describe if you want them to turn off the AC or turn the heat down when they're away

6. House How-to Instructions

Consider this the troubleshooting section of your House Manual. Anticipate any potential problems your guests may have before they have a chance to arise and leave clear instructions for the best way to deal with them.

If your guests can't figure out how to use things, it may affect their review. So, make sure to include helpful information and how-to instructions that are easy to understand.

For instance, give instructions on how to use kitchen appliances. Some of these appliances might seem like common sense to operate but understand that not all of your guests may have used these before or may have used a different model that operates much differently.

Leave simple operating instructions and information for things items such as:

- Heating and cooling units
- Thermostat
- Fireplace
- Barbecue
- Swimming pool or hot tub
- Washer and dryer

Providing instructions here will prevent you from receiving phone calls at odd hours from frustrated guests.

Make sure to explain any smart technology you may have in the home including:

- Smart TV and remote control
- Netflix/HBO/Hulu
- Alexa
- Smart bulbs

You can even mention any quirks of your STR in this section, such as if your Wi-Fi works well inside the house but not as well on the back deck.

7. Local Ordinances and Rules

Making your guests aware of local ordinances and rules is essential for avoiding problems with their stay. Mention if your area has specific local regulations, for example, some areas prohibit campfires or fireworks, and certain areas require their trash to be contained in a locked trash bin.

8. Local Recommendations and Places of Interest

Viewing your rental through your TIG's eyes will help you better understand what information would be helpful for them. But the main goal here is making your property's location shine.

Your guests expect you to be a trusted hometown authority, and guests value personal recommendations. Describe what makes your locale so special.

Are there any local traditions, festivals, or tourist attractions? What other activities or attractions does your area offer?

Demonstrate your expertise in the area and consider what parts of town your guests might like, such as a farmer's market, a secret sunset lookout point, or the best places for photo opportunities.

Show off your expertise and try to suggest a variety of things to do. Include a range of things such as outdoor adventures or fun activities for the whole family. Include more leisurely activities such as walks or hikes in the area, bike paths, or second-hand markets.

Let them know how many fun things they have at their disposal. Guests will appreciate this and will be more likely to leave you a 5-star review.

9. Restaurants, Bars, and Nightlife

Guests appreciate getting insider tips on hidden gems and local favorites. This section should offer recommendations of all the wonderful restaurant and cafe choices nearby. Then organize them by type of cuisine and price, and make sure to include gluten-free and vegan options.

Mention if there is a style of cooking unique to your area. Or perhaps suggest a popular drink, or meal that everyone must try.

Highlight any well-known restaurants or must-visit eateries in your area. List any swanky wine bars or nightlife locations your guests may want to check out. But remember that not all your guests may drink alcohol, so try to include non-alcoholic places as well, like smoothie and juice bars or even food markets.

Lastly, feel free to highlight your personal favorites along with recommended dishes to try at these restaurants. Don't forget to include a phone number and a website or link to make reservations. It's also nice to include a map to help guests find them easier. They'll be grateful to have insider tips.

10. Additional Suggestions

Remember that guests will likely be unfamiliar with the local surroundings, so adding a list of useful stores and shops will save them time and can help them find what they need. Include things like:

- The closest grocery store
- Local shopping malls
- 24-hour convenience stores

- Gas stations
- Pharmacies
- Nearby gyms
- ATMs and bank tellers
- Local religious sites and places of worship

11. Transportation Information

Create a section with tips on how to get around your area. It also helps to share any shortcuts that only locals would know.

Provide phone numbers and schedules that could be useful to your guests, such as:

- Taxi and shuttle services
- Bus routes—include bus and train timetables or include links to online schedules
- Car rentals
- Airports and train stations

Provide a map of the area showing directions to the nearest:

- Airport
- Bus station
- Train station

This information is extremely helpful, especially if your STR is off-the-grid, where one may not necessarily have access to cell service.

12. Special Touches

Don't miss out on the opportunity to make your guests feel special. Pick from these ideas or come up with your own:

- Mention that you've left a bottle of wine for their pleasure

INSTRUCTION OVERLOAD

- Leave a voucher for a fresh cup of coffee at the cafe down the street
- Offer a discount code for the next time they book a trip through your website

Or include a personalized section for your TIG and include anything that would apply to them specifically.

For example, if you're hosting honeymooners, you can have a special section for them, including things like:

- Contact information of honeymoon photographers
- Best romantic dining spots
- Best place for a couples massage

The same could be done for a family reunion, a bachelor party, or a birthday celebration. Customizing your House Manual and adding a few hand-selected favorites is sure to be a hit for your guests.

13. Contact Information for Future Correspondence

Ensure your guests know exactly how to reach you after their stay, especially if they made reservations through an OTA or third-party site.

In addition, ask them to join your mailing list so they can receive property updates and discounts. It's also a good idea to provide a link to your social media accounts.

There are so many options when creating a House Manual for your guests. Regardless of what you choose to add, make it welcoming and informative.

After all, happy guests tend to rebook, take better care of your home, and leave 5-star reviews.

5-STAR HOST'R ACTION PLAN

1. Follow the design hot tips
2. Put together your House Manual

SECTION 2
Renting Out The Entire House

For those of you STR Hosts renting out an entire house, you will find extra things to consider.

In some cases, you will have a larger area with more rooms and space to furnish, while in other cases, you may have a vacation destination where you can provide alluring amenities to really shine.

If you are through your trial-and-error phase and have decided to make your STR a business instead of a hobby, it may also make sense for you to consider expanding beyond the online travel portals to your own direct booking site.

Each of these scenarios will be discussed in this section.

But no matter where you are in your journey, make sure to follow my Key Takeaways and then absorb the information in the 5-Star Host'r Way section.

Lastly, implement what serves you from the Action Plan to sustain a steady stream of 5-star reviews.

Chapter 5

BOOKING BARE MINIMUM

They should've known when they found this listing online for a bargain price that it was too good to be true!

My sister and her family live in Pittsburgh, Pennsylvania, where it gets cold and dreary. Therefore, they always like to plan a trip away to someplace warm in the springtime. This particular year, they decided to head to the beach in North Carolina.

My sister loves to pick out just the right place for her family to stay, so she scoured through dozens and dozens of vacation rentals and really did her research. Her husband's one request was that he wanted "toes in the sand." In other words, he wanted to walk out his back door straight onto the sandy beach and then run a few feet to jump in the waves.

But as she would soon find out, most of the houses on the beach of the Outer Banks were really expensive to rent and, unfortunately, were out of their price range.

Just as she was beginning to think that getting a house on the beach was out of reach for them, she came across what looked to be a true gem and was surprisingly affordable.

It was big enough to house her family of five comfortably, and it had multiple patio doors and picture windows providing wonderful ocean views. Best of all, it had a large deck off the back where they could relax and have dinners, and it was just a hop and a step into the water.

Although she knew they might get what they paid for, when they arrived, they realized it was way worse than what they expected.

The first unpleasant surprise was that the beds were stripped down to the mattress, and they could not find any sheets or towels. I mean, not a one!

So, my sister sent a text to the owner, and he very rudely wrote back and said, "Sheets and towels are not included. Did you not get my email?"

And she replied promptly, "You never sent me an email."

He replied, "Well, you'll need to go out and buy some." But it was late in the evening when they arrived, and at that point, all the stores were closed.

Unfortunately, the first night they had to sleep on some old beach towels they had brought with them. And the next day, they spent over $200 on new sheet sets and blankets.

The second problem with the house was that it leaked. They could tell right when they walked in and were greeted with a musty stench that something was wrong.

Sadly, on that first night, a large thunderstorm rolled in. And I'm not talking a gentle rain. No, it was pouring rain and continued for three consecutive days of their stay.

And you've probably guessed it by now—the very first night, as they were trying to fall asleep under their beach towels, they heard drip, drip, drip. Sure enough, every sliding glass door—four sets in fact—all leaked.

Drip, drip, drip.

And I don't mean a small drip. I mean enough that they gathered all the Tupperware containers in the kitchen and put them under every drip. The containers were half full by the first morning, so they emptied them. But then they had to continuously empty those Tupperware containers every day for the next three days.

Now, this was obviously not the first time leaks had occurred because when they walked in, they smelled that moldy, musty stench of wet carpet. So, they opened all the windows right away to air out the house, but once the rain started, they had to shut the windows and doors and live with that odor.

At this point, my sister thought this was important enough to text the landlord again to let him know about all the leaks. Again, he rudely replied, "I don't have time to write to you. My wife has left me, I haven't had dinner, and I've been driving all day."

Clearly, this rental was not his primary residence. He was not living in it currently. Nor did it seem he checked on it often. It was a wreck.

I wondered, "How could this owner not take care of this beautiful home? Why didn't he seem to care about the condition of the property? Why didn't he care about the comfort of his guests and what type of review he might receive?"

My guess is that his personal life was falling apart and he had the same lackluster attitude toward his property and his guests. I assume that he figured he had the least expensive rental on the beach and that most people were coming for the beach. But this does not hold true when you're stuck inside for half of your vacation due to inclement weather.

Oh, brother! The location was so perfect. It was toes in the sand, right on the beach.

They tried to convince themselves that although they had to endure three consecutive days of rain, at least they had a fantastic view of the ocean outside the huge picture window. Even though it was overcast and dreary out, they were looking at the ocean, the waves and the sand and the location was so awesome. But that didn't change the wrecked nature of the house.

My sister sighed as she remembered the situation and said, "Actually, his deck was also a mess, and we spent about an hour or two sweeping, hosing it down, and getting rid of all the sand and mossy stuff on it. We even scrubbed it with a brush."

Apparently, that deck was really nice by the time they finished cleaning it.

It's troublesome to think that they would have to go to those efforts just to utilize the deck. But they wanted to eat out there once the rain subsided and they couldn't stomach the thought of sitting out there because it was in such bad shape.

Sadly, the story does not end here.

Not only was this host extremely rude, but it was also clear that he was not cut out for the Airbnb business.

I inquired, "Did he at least provide the basics?"

It turns out he did not even offer the basic expected supplies—soap, paper towels, or toilet paper. He didn't have anything. He offered literally *nothing* that a guest would expect to have at an STR.

Imagine arriving late at night to your rental beach home. You're exhausted from traveling all day; all you want to do is take a warm shower and go to bed. None of that was possible!

Then I asked, "Did he provide a House Manual that gave instructions or provided you with suggestions for where to shop or eat in the area?"

She replied, "Oh my goodness, no. No manual, and no welcome anything. No food, no basket. I'm telling you, there was nothing!"

I also asked if he provided any beach towels or beach paraphernalia.

She chuckled at the thought, "No, but luckily we brought our own beach gear because we drove. We brought our own chairs. We brought our own umbrellas. And fortunately, we brought our own beach towels and sunscreen."

At this point, I could tell my sister was getting riled up having to relive this vacation, but I was dying to know. "What about Internet service?" I asked.

She scoffed, "Oh, the Internet was terrible. We couldn't get online with the password he provided, so I had to text him again, and again he rudely wrote back, "It's the best on the island." In other words, "figure it out yourself!"

This story was getting better and better, and she seemed willing to talk about it, so I asked, "Did you have to do any chores for him?"

"Well, of course, we had to put the trash out. Oh, and this guy had the worst contract I've ever seen. Worst, meaning he had the most rules. He had a whole page explaining how to put the trash out. And by the way, the trash was under his carport, and the street was about a hundred yards off a dirt driveway. But by the time you had three days of rain, it was mud. So literally, we were dragging four bins to the street because the guy before us hadn't remembered to remove his trash, so there was already trash in several of the bins. And wouldn't you guess that when we were there, it was trash day. We had to drag these four bins through the mud to the street, and each bin had a number on it. And he was very specific in his directions."

He spelled out, "Here are the numbers of my bins. And if these bins are not returned to the exact spot where you got them in the carport, you'll be charged $100 per bin."

Unbelievable! Why would this guy care if they were in numeric order or not, as long as they got returned to their spot?

She continued, "Yeah. Everything had a hundred-dollar fine. If you don't do this, you get charged a hundred dollars. If you don't do that, you get charged a hundred dollars. He had a whole long list. And I don't remember how he was going to charge us. He was all about penalties. And then in his cupboards, he had it all spelled out, 'There are five wine glasses, there are six mugs.' And if I recall correctly, his rules said, 'If there are any glasses, mugs, or silverware missing, you'll be charged a hundred dollars.' Like seriously. He had a whole list of penalties. Coercion at its finest!"

She continued, "He just should have given us a heads up. He was simply a bad landlord. The location was great, and we would otherwise not have been on the beach because we weren't willing to spend that kind of money to be on the beach."

"Oh, wow," I said, "and what did you end up doing with the sheets and towels you bought?"

She said, "We brought them home. And actually, we use them. But we didn't need them; they're extra. But if he had actually told me ahead of time, like he thought he had, I would have brought some from home."

Fact: Location, location, location does not always hold true! This owner simply did not take care of his property and did not care about his guests.

REVIEW: 3 out of 5 stars

At this point, I had to know, "and the review you gave?"

My sister replied, "So I gave him a 3-star review: Five for location, one for service, three overall. And though I might have given a lower rating, I thought that was quite fair, actually. He reviewed me and gave me three stars, with no comments."

I balked, "just like out of spite?"

She responded, "Yeah. Basically. Either out of spite or he didn't like that I texted him. In reality, I only sent maybe three or four texts. Just once or twice about the sheets and towels, to understand where I was supposed to go shopping. Then once about the drips, really out of courtesy, to let him know that we were taking care of his leaks because otherwise, the carpet would've been completely ruined. And we knew that when we left, no guests were staying after us. So, I texted when we were leaving to ask him if we should leave the Tupperware containers out because he might not want those drips to be on the carpet. And he said, 'No, please wash them and return them to the kitchen where you got them.'"

I was in total and utter shock and said, "Wow. So not even the cleaning person was going to clean the Tupperware? You had to?"

She sighed deeply and replied, "Yeah."

KEY TAKEAWAYS AND DESIGN HOT TIPS

1. Provide your guests with basic essentials such as soap, toilet paper, paper towels, spices, etcetera.
2. Guests expect an STR to include sheets, blankets, pillows and towels. If you are not providing these, make it clear in your listing. Guests need to be aware of this ahead of time to make other arrangements.
3. Make sure your property is thoroughly cleaned inside and out before each new booking.
4. Make needed repairs as they occur and have a plan for quick repairs while guests are staying at your property.
5. Do not add on silly, unnecessary charges for items that may accidentally break, such as dishware and glasses. This is part of your business expense.
6. Treat guests courteously if they contact you with questions while they are staying at your property. And as mentioned in Chapter 4, consider putting together a House Manual that explains how things work in the house.

THE 5-STAR HOST'R WAY—ESSENTIALS PER ROOM

When running a successful STR, you always want to make the property as homelike and comfortable as possible, starting from the moment you enter the home.

Here are the essentials required for each room—if applicable:

Front Door

- Ring doorbell with camera—ensures only paid guests are accessing your propert
- Lockbox or keyless entry—select one that provides temporary codes to prevent unauthorized access

- Security lights—for late-night arrivals

Entry

- Hooks or coat rack—if no nearby coat closet
- Umbrella rack—if applicable for climate
- Entry table if there is room—this provides a great place for your House Manual and a place to set the keys
- Rug or runner in front of the door
- Artwork and decor

Living Room

- Comfortable seating—to fit the number of guests allowed
- Throw pillows to add pops of color
- Coffee table
- Side tables
- Lamps with adequate lighting for each seating area—USB plugins are a plus
- Smart TV with streaming options
- Rug—if hard surface flooring
- Artwork and decor
- Experience items—games, books, puzzles, etcetera

Kitchen

- Breakfast table—size to fit the number of guests allowed
- Kitchen chairs—to fit the number of guests allowed
- Stools for a breakfast bar, if applicable

Dining Room

- Table—size to fit number of guests allowed
- Dining chairs—to fit the number of guests allowed

- Rug—if hard surface flooring
- Placemats and table runner to prevent wear and tear
- Centerpiece for the table
- Artwork
- Shelving or buffet, if adequate space

Bedroom
- Bedframe and mattress
- Comfortable mattress pad—not vinyl
- Three sheet sets per bed
- Two pillows of various firmness per person—with an extra set in the closet
- Pillow covers—to protect pillows from wear and tear
- Blankets
- Comforter
- Throw pillows and throw blanket—to add a pop of color
- Nightstand for each side of the bed—only one needed for twin beds
- USB lamps—add reading lights, if needed
- Dresser or chest of drawers
- Full-length mirror
- Plenty of hangers
- Luggage racks—two per room
- Trash can
- Smart TV—in primary bedroom, if space allows
- Chair or bench if adequate space
- Rug—if hard surface flooring
- Artwork and décor

Bathroom
- Two towel sets per guest, including bath and hand towels, and wash cloth—with extra set in closet
- Shower curtain with a mold-resistant liner if applicable
- Bathroom scale
- Bath rug—if hard surface flooring
- Artwork
- Toiletries

Miscellaneous Spaces

Identify what each room is or what it can be used for. For example:

Office
- Desk
- Desk chair
- Shelving
- Printer
- Artwork

Theater Room
- Movie projector and screen
- Seating
- Popcorn maker

Game Room
- Pool table
- Game table with chairs
- Bar height table
- Bar chairs

Exterior

- Outdoor table—size to fit the number of guests allowed
- Outdoor chairs—to fit the number of guests allowed
- Umbrella for shade
- Lounge chairs
- Gas grill

Bonus:

One of the biggest appeals of STR travel is that it allows guests to cook their own meals, thereby avoiding overpriced and unhealthy restaurant fare.

Providing a wide array of cooking utensils and kitchen essentials, welcomes your guests in style and helps them feel right at home.

For a Basic Essentials list when furnishing a kitchen, bathroom and utility closet visit: https://The5-StarHost.com/Essentials

5-STAR HOST'R ACTION PLAN

1. Follow the design hot tips.
2. Confirm you are properly equipped in each room of your property with the essentials.
3. Grab the Basic Essentials list above and furnish your property with anything missing from that list.

Chapter 6

SOMEONE GOT IT RIGHT!

It was that time of year again. My husband and I always take an annual birthday trip to somewhere tropical. Our birthdays happen to be only three days apart; therefore, we get to celebrate our birthdays together.

We were about to hit the one-year mark for COVID-19, and decided it was safer to stay in the United States. So, we chose to go back to Siesta Key, Florida, for a week.

But as I mentioned in Chapter 3, we were not about to go back to the Beach Bungalow. We knew better than to repeat that nightmare!

My husband wanted to stay right on the beach, and he was not having much luck finding anything on Airbnb. So, he decided to look through VRBO.

What he found turned out to be an absolute gem.

This one bedroom/one bathroom unit was in a quiet condo development located between the pier and the beach.

As with the Beach Bungalow, this place also had access to a private beach. It was about a half mile down from where we had stayed before. But the beach was the same powdered sugar sand that melted under your toes and never got hot.

The kitchen in this condo had recently been remodeled, and the bathroom provided adequate space for our toiletries.

It was clear this unit was used strictly for an STR and not as a permanent residence. Consequently, we had plenty of space in the closet for our clothes, and the drawers were all empty. We even had room in the closet to store our empty suitcases. What a novel idea, huh?

We were delighted to find an outstanding House Manual with all the information that we could possibly need. From the Wi-Fi password to her favorite places to eat. It was clear, concise, and informational. No fluff.

She provided easy yet very specific instructions on how to reach the private beach. Beside the House Manual sat a set of keys that gave us access to the locked gate for the beach entry. It was tricky, but she made it so clear that we did not have any issues.

Additionally, she left us instructions on how to access various apps on her TV. This was super helpful, as we've had difficulties with this in many places we've stayed before, and my husband has little patience for this type of thing.

This rental happened to be one of the most comfortable places we have stayed in to date. Although it was a small condo unit, it had everything we needed.

The kitchen was fully stocked. She had everything from cooking utensils to fully stocked spices to a toaster and even a blender.

She had the cutest coffee area set up for us. It was as if we were in a Starbucks, and we could prepare whatever we wanted at a whim.

She had literally thought through every detail for us. The bathroom was stocked with toiletries, even though we had brought our own. She had extra sets of fluffy towels for us. And she provided shelves for us to place the toiletries we had brought.

The bedroom was an adequate size, so we were not tripping over ourselves and our belongings.

SOMEONE GOT IT RIGHT!

The king bed was incredibly comfortable. So much so that we did not want to get out of bed in the morning. Now, that sounds like a vacation, right?

There was a little back patio off the bedroom where we drank our coffee in the morning.

But one of the greatest surprises we found at this property was all of the beach paraphernalia that she provided.

She had a wagon set up with beach chairs and an umbrella—all of which actually worked.

She also provided us with various coolers if we wanted to bring cold beverages to the beach with us.

In addition, she provided quite an array of large, fluffy beach towels. She even left us several bottles of sunscreen and aloe vera to cool our tender sunburnt skin.

This VRBO host seemed to have thought of everything for us. As I've suggested in past chapters, she anticipated our every need before we even knew we would need these things.

She understood that the majority of her guests were traveling from afar and coming to her place for a beach vacation. Therefore, she knew well what would be needed for that particular type of guest—her TIG.

To carry out the theme, her property was decorated with many beach-type artifacts and artwork. It was tastefully done. Not too over the top, and it was obvious that she carefully planned this design with her guests in mind.

This particular host provided just the right amount of communication and never bothered us throughout our stay. She had easy check-in and check-out procedures and did not request us to do any chores for her.

As a good 5-Star Host'r would do, she had a cleaning crew that arrived after our departure to handle all cleaning procedures. As opposed to the Beach Bungalow, we were not expected to do any of the cleaning. What a relief—our previous experience was not a "Siesta Key thing;" it was a "Beach Bungalow thing!"

What a difference from our first stay in Siesta Key. Now, this is the proper way to run an STR business.

This is a place that we would definitely return to again, and unlike our first accommodations, we would highly recommend this VRBO to anyone wanting to visit Siesta Key.

REVIEW: This was a no-brainer. **5 out of 5 stars.** We couldn't have asked for anything more.

KEY TAKEAWAYS AND DESIGN HOT TIPS

Everything about this STR is a perfect example to follow to become a 5-Star Host'r. Here is what this host did starting from the beginning:

1. Chose her targeted ideal client—TIG, based on her location, near the beach, and planned everything around her TIG
2. Check-in and check-out procedures were seamless
3. Provided brochures of fun things to do in the area and included a list of her favorite restaurants and their locations
4. Stocked the refrigerator with ice-cold bottles of water for the taking
5. Provided a House Manual/Welcome Book with all the pertinent information
6. Offered very clear instructions on how to use her Smart TV
7. Provided clear instructions on how to enter the gate to the private beach; she even told us where to store the keys upon our return so that we would always know where they were
8. Offered all of the essentials we could have wanted in the kitchen, including a blender for frozen drinks
9. Designed her property with a cohesive beach theme throughout, including comfortable furniture and paint

colors, plus tasteful beach artifacts and artwork; nothing was overdone

10. Dedicated an outdoor set up for relaxing
11. Provided all the possible beach amenities one could hope for, including beach chairs, an umbrella, various coolers for to keep our food and drinks cold, a wagon to tote all of this to the beach, a variety of beach towels, sunscreen, and aloe vera to sooth our sunburns
12. Bathroom was stocked with toiletries, should we have needed them
13. Did not bother us during our stay, but we knew she was available should we need anything
14. Did not expect us to do chores for her
15. Hired a cleaning crew to handle all the cleaning instead of expecting us to pitch in

Everything was done perfectly with her TIG in mind. Kudos to this host!

THE 5-STAR HOST'R WAY—ALLURING AMENITIES

Providing alluring amenities is an exceptional way to set yourself apart from your competition and gain more bookings, as well as those coveted 5-star reviews.

The good news is that this step should be easy for you, assuming you have already honed in on your TIG. Now comes the fun part, where you can begin to plan out what alluring amenities to offer as you draw TIGs in.

But before we dive into planning your amenities package, let's take a look at the top ten amenities guests want right now—according to Airbnb's search results worldwide:

1. A pool
2. Wi-Fi
3. A kitchen
4. Free parking
5. A jacuzzi
6. A washer or dryer
7. Air conditioning or heating
8. Self-check-in
9. Laptop-friendly workspace
10. Pets allowed

This does not mean that you should go out and spend the money to add a pool to your backyard! The list is simply a place to start. But the key is knowing your TIG so well that you know what amenities will make their stay unique.

Step 1: Basic Amenity Practices

It's essential to work with what you have. Do not choose amenities for everyone on earth. Mass appeal is dead.

Follow these initial steps to get started:

1. **Know Your Market**

    Start by taking some time to become familiar with local amenities, as well as any new competition that may have an impact on the success of your STR.

2. **Research Your Hotel and STR Competition**

    Conduct online research to find details about other STR properties and hotels in the area, particularly any upgrades they have made or special features they offer.

3. **Define What Makes Your Property Different and What Elements Set You Apart**

    See if there is something that can differentiate your place from your competition. Consider the following:

SOMEONE GOT IT RIGHT!

- What makes your property unique or different—perhaps it's smaller or larger than your competition
- Is your property located within walking distance of special attractions—make sure to mention that and specify a travel time frame along with a copy of a Google map
- Is your space in an HOA that provides access to a swimming pool or a gym—mention this
- Is your area best suited for young singles—offer a one-week gym pass or a gift certificate to the nearby Starbucks
- Does your space cater to families with small babies—you could provide a Pack 'N Play, baby monitor, and a high chair
- Do you allow pets—perhaps you want to include a pet walking service
- Are you simply renting out a bedroom in your house—offer the best gourmet breakfast in town

4. **What Experiences Would Your TIG Love**

   Ask yourself these questions and be really honest with your answers, knowing that there are no wrong answers.

   - If I were to rent a space in my area, what would I be looking for, and what added services would be the tipping point?
   - Is my property geared for romance?
   - Is my property at a vacation destination like a beach house, lake cottage or mountain lodge?
   - Am I set up for the business traveler?
   - Is my property off-the-grid—with no Wi-Fi available—for a true unplugged vacation?

5. **What Do You Want Your TIG to *Feel* as a Result of Their Stay**
    - What are people coming for?
    - Are they coming to experience something different?
    - What feeling are they seeking?

Example 1: For the nostalgic TIG—rural life on a farm with a lemonade stand or fresh eggs in a bowl

Example 2: For the Eco-conscious TIG—focus on the carbon footprint and reducing waste

Step 2: General Amenity Tip

Thoughtful amenities can distinguish between an awesome trip or a surprisingly frustrating one. But let's go a step above and design an alluring amenities package specifically for your TIG:

1. Start at the Beginning

Help your TIGs with their arrival. Think about these possible scenarios that would be beneficial to your TIG.

When I think about why I like destination vacations so much, it occurs to me that they make it easy for the traveler to get around.

For instance, when traveling to Mexico, they include transfers from the airport to your resort. This is either included in the price of the vacation package, or it is an added fee. In either case, it is a relief not to worry about grabbing a bus or cab in a foreign country.

The same should hold true for your STR. Make it easy for your guests to arrive at your property.

Many guests will be coming from out of state and arriving by plane and may not be familiar with your area and all of the different routes to get to your property.

Consider the different ways guests will arrive and provide a service to help in any situation. For instance:

- Airport pick-up and drop-off—can be included in the STR price or as an add-on fee
- City transfers
- Rental car locations
- Uber or Lyft services
- Chauffeur services
- Sightseeing tours
- Provide directions to your STR, or suggest the best ways to use public transportation
- If construction is happening in your neighborhood or if parking options are limited, give guests a heads-up, and provide alternatives

2. Provide Local Pointers

This is your city and your space, so you know how to highlight it best. Think about what your TIG will be doing while at your property and location and add more benefits such as:

- List of your favorite restaurants nearby
- Maps or guidebooks
- Retail recommendations
- Share insider tips
- Offer suggestions on things to do in the area
- Create an inclusive and engaging guidebook to give guests local tips that focus on your city and your hospitality

3. Provide Comfort Amenities to Make Their Stay More Memorable

When it comes to creating an attractive amenities package, it's not always about having a luxury property or expensive, high-end amenities. The small gestures add a personal touch to make a guest's stay even more comfortable and memorable:

- Go above and beyond by leaving wine and chocolates
- Arrange fresh flowers for each stay
- Add a coffee bar *and* waffle bar
- Leave your favorite local coffee and let them know where they can buy more
- Put together a welcome basket of goodies to fill weary guest's bellies after a long day of traveling
- Furnish luggage racks in each bedroom for the guest's suitcases
- Make sure you have plenty of extras on hand—towels, bedding, toilet paper, makeup wipes, soap, shampoo, paper towels, cleaning supplies
- Provide bedside chargers
- Add luxury by providing comfy white terry cloth robes

4. Local Flair

Part of the joy of staying at an STR is discovering the local flair, such as distinctive flavors scents, sights, and noises of a new location. It's a nice gesture to share some of these things with your guests:

- Add local flair: Provide flowers from your garden, local honey, jams, or fresh fruit and veggies from the local farmer's market
- Think regionally: Provide local craft brews; leave brochures, local magazines, and books about the city

- Tailor the experience: Provide local delicacies to celebrate a birthday
- Build relationships with nearby restaurant owners: Offer your guests a discount for their anniversary or birthday dinner celebration

5. Experiences

An experience is something your guest will remember doing while at your place, which equates to word-of-mouth referrals and return guests. Get inside the mind of your TIG and think of the best possible experiences to offer them. For instance:

- Beach: Provide a beach kit with chairs, an umbrella, an ice chest, children's toys, sunscreen, and a wagon
- Mountainous area: Offer ski rentals and provide snowshoes, or binoculars and fishing poles
- Family-friendly: Provide a craft cabinet to make friendship bracelets, picture frames, etcetera, and leave a deck of cards and games they can enjoy as a family
- Couples retreat: Offer a free romantic dinner at a nearby restaurant
- Business traveler: Include a workspace area, high-speed Internet, a printer, and office supplies
- Outdoor living: Provide mosquito repellent and citronella candles
- Keep your local climate in mind: Provide disposable rain ponchos and umbrellas in a rainy climate

Step 3: Specific Category Amenity Examples

Now, let's look at five specific categories and brainstorm a little deeper on what they may need.

1. Remote Business Workers

COVID-19 certainly increased the numbers of remote workers, and many of these folks chose to work from new locations or different cities. By offering certain amenities, you can help meet their needs:

- Reliable Wi-Fi: Fast Internet speeds are a must for remote workers
- A well-lit workspace: Locate a desk or table near a power source, with a comfortable ergonomic chair and plenty of light
- Office supplies: Simple items like ball-point pens, notepads, a stapler, scotch tape, and a stack of sticky notes often come in handy
- Tech necessities: Provide a computer monitor they can hook their laptop into, smart speakers, a color printer, and copy paper
- Extras: Provide surge protectors, headphones, and extra chargers
- Video conferencing backdrop: Add appealing backdrops for guests who are frequently on video calls, such as interesting wallpaper or art situated in the background of a workspace
- Noise reduction: Soft goods like curtains, throw rugs, blankets, and pillows can help soften noisy distractions

2. Seniors

Senior travelers with limited mobility or unique access needs are becoming more prevalent as the baby boomers age. In this case, create a world where everyone can feel welcome by providing helpful information such as:

- Identify which restaurants in the area have ramps
- Provide a list of walking trails that have paved pathways

- Note which museums have plenty of parking close to the entrance

To help you stand out to senior guests, showcase the following accessibility features in your listing:

- Flat terrain leading to the front door with no steep inclines
- High voltage lighting on pathways to the entrance
- Accessible parking spot
- Step-free entry and entryways to rooms
- Wide entryways to access rooms
- Walk-in shower
- Shower and toilet grab bars
- Shower chair

3. ADA Compliant

This is an untapped and much-needed market that you may want to consider.

Here are a few items you can install in your property to make it ADA compliant:

- Wheelchair or handicap accessible
- Thirty-two-inch doorways and shower opening
- Roll-in shower with handheld extension for shower head
- Twenty-five-inch standard height bed
- Three-inch clearance under sofa and bed
- Portable ramps from Walmart for several steps
- Not super fluffy carpet
- Plates and cups on a lower level or in a drawer
- Tables at thirty inches, so knees fit under
- Grab bars—Sea Chrome has stylish grab bars

- Switch door knobs into handles

4. Pet Friendly

Many guests these days want to bring their pets with them on trips. In fact, according to TripAdvisor, 53 percent of pet owners travel with their pets. If you don't accept pets, that's a missed opportunity.

If at all possible, make your STR pet friendly to stand out from the competition. Further statistics report that travelers with pets stay longer and are more likely to leave positive reviews.

Guests traveling with pets will need to know whether you have an enclosed patio or a fenced-in yard. But here are some additional great pet-friendly amenities that you can provide:

- Water and food bowls for pets
- Pet-friendly furniture covers
- Designated towels to wipe off paws at the door
- Pet bedding and toys
- Leashes
- Scratching post and litter box, if you allow cats
- Extra cleaning supplies

5. Families with Kids

Parents with small children have difficulty traveling with all the needed supplies. You can **help them feel** more comfortable in your space by supplying some of the things they need most, such as:

- Cribs
- Changing table
- Pack 'N Play
- Highchairs
- Kid's cups, plates, and utensils

SOMEONE GOT IT RIGHT!

- Baby monitors
- Baby gates
- Outlet covers

Remember, the more specific you are with your TIG and service offerings, the more your bookings will grow.

If you are still unsure of your amenities package, staying in your space for a night or two to experience it as a guest offers tremendous insight.

Beyond that, make sure to pay close attention to your guests' feedback because they will offer up ideas you might not have thought of on your own.

Over time, you'll figure out the best amenities package that will take your listing to the next level, make your guest's stay more memorable, and of course, bring on those 5-star reviews.

5-STAR HOST'R ACTION PLAN

1. Follow the design hot tips
2. Follow the first two steps from the 5-Star Host'r Way section to fine-tune your alluring amenities package

Chapter 7

PRICE GOUGING WITH A TWIST

My family had all survived COVID-19 for the past fifteen months, and although we may have been ready to return to normal, the world was not.

During this time of the world being in chaos, my remarkable twin nieces completed all of their undergraduate requirements and were prepared to graduate from Stanford University. As proud family members, we were eager to celebrate them and their astounding accomplishments.

So, three months before the celebration, we began our travel plans. After being stuck at home for the past fifteen months, travel bans were beginning to ease up. We were coming from all over the country to gather for this glorious event, and we were relieved to have the option to fly instead of drive for days.

Excellent! We all had our various flights booked. Step one was complete, and it felt as though things were coming together.

Shortly after we all booked our flights, we learned Stanford was limiting the number of tickets allotted to each student. COVID-19 was still a huge concern, and although the graduation ceremony was going to be held in the outdoor stadium, each student was allowed only two tickets.

Unfortunately, eight of us were going to the celebration, so only four of us would be allowed in. The rest of us would have to watch the streaming ceremony on our laptops.

Ok, so we could deal with this. We decided who would attend in-person and who would sit outside the stadium and watch on our phones. I was a part of the phone group but still thrilled to be a part of what I could.

Great, step two complete. Check!

Now, we needed to find accommodations.

As a group, we agreed it would be nice to all stay in one large house so we wouldn't have to worry about wearing masks and reduce the risk of catching COVID-19.

We all started scouring various travel portals for the perfect place.

My sister, the twins' mother, found several very nice large houses and sent each listing to all of us to review and vote on which one we liked best.

The group made a unanimous decision, so she booked it.

The place she booked seemed perfect for our extended family celebration. It had a large backyard with a volleyball net, a firepit, and a large deck with lots of room for an outdoor party. It also had an immense kitchen and dining room that would easily house our planned celebration. Best of all, it had five bedrooms and four bathrooms. Perfect for our group of eight. This was an amazing find, and we were all very excited about the upcoming trip.

Throughout the next month, we began making our plans for various gatherings at this amazing house. We planned a luncheon with some of the girls' classmates and, of course, a party and celebratory dinner following the big event. Invitations went out, and RSVPs were tallied.

Perfect, step three complete! Or so we thought…

Sadly, just six weeks before the graduation, the owner of the Airbnb we had booked wrote my sister and told her that their plans had

PRICE GOUGING WITH A TWIST

changed. They said their own family was visiting them from out of state, and they needed their house for their own family gathering.

He canceled— just like that!! Is that even legal?

Apparently so. The owner took our beautiful accommodations right out from under us at what felt like the last minute. We were left whirling in disbelief! What were we going to do? All the larger homes were now booked, and we were left with slim pickings.

Nonetheless, we began the laborious task of searching for hotel suites that could house all of us, and we were coming up short.

Then, my sister remembered that we had a backup property that we were considering, but it only had four bedrooms and two bathrooms. She looked it up again on Airbnb, and lo and behold, it was still available for the week we needed it.

But as she looked more closely, she realized that it had doubled in price since we were first considering it.

Wait, what? Are they allowed to do that??

Isn't that considered price gouging?

The problem is that the locals knew that people were coming in from all over the world to attend this graduation, and they felt they could raise their prices for the week.

Alas, what could we do? We had to have a place to stay.

So, she booked this second option and, after waiting several hours, received the following response, "I apologize, but my place should have been unlisted, and there was a glitch on the system as it is not currently available to rent. My apologies."

My sister exclaimed to me, "Why was it even listed as available? I'm beginning to lose faith in Airbnb."

So, of course, I was curious if she had only searched on Airbnb or if she had searched a variety of other travel platforms as well.

She stated, "Yes, I've spent hours scouring VRBO and every other available rental site—there are a bunch!"

She continued, "There are a few places available in the Bay Area, but it's just that none are as good as what we had, so we will need to compromise on something—either less space, or worse neighborhood, or no backyard, or more money, or farther away—or a combination of all of those."

She explained that she had devised a very detailed spreadsheet of all possible STRs with a separate column for all the ones she had reached out to and put a deposit on. At one point, she had deposits out to five different properties that had all fallen through and was beginning to worry about getting all of her deposits back. Spoiler: fortunately, they were all returned in full.

She added, "I have tried, and tried but unfortunately, I cannot find a nice house where we all will fit. My suggestion is we rent a smaller house from Thursday to Tuesday in the Stanford area where we can all hang out together. A portion of us will sleep in this house and the others can stay somewhere else nearby to sleep."

It was much easier to find availability at hotels with single rooms, as well as many smaller Airbnb rentals with one or two bedrooms. This came as a relief.

As we all began to make different arrangements, we heard from my sister again.

"Big turn of events this morning! I was getting discouraged after I heard back from two different places that they had doubled their rates because of Stanford graduation. But then, suddenly, like a miracle, this house that I have never seen listed before popped into my feed. The title caught my eye."

She immediately sent in a request, expecting it to be declined like so many others she had tried in the past few days, but this one was immediately accepted!!

She explained that we had forty-eight hours to cancel if anyone should find a reason proving this was too good to be true!

But, shortly after she reached out to us, the host responded to my sister about the booking, "Apologies as my advertised rates were incorrect. I had updated the listing but forgot to update Airbnb.

PRICE GOUGING WITH A TWIST

I'll do that now; if you'd like to book, you can proceed in doing so. Sorry about the inconvenience."

WHAT?? How is it possible for *all* of these hosts to be pulling the rug out from under us? We were appalled!

We had to decline her offer because we could not afford her new rates.

Back to the drawing board.

At this point, my sister decided to take a chance and wrote to the owners of the second place we were looking at to see if they would honor their original price. She explained what had happened with the previous hosts and relayed our current predicament.

Fortunately, the woman responded quickly and offered to honor their original price. Her one caveat was that it had to be a "direct booking" and not through Airbnb. She explained that it would benefit both parties because there would be no Airbnb fees.

"It occurred to us that you may prefer to have a direct transaction and avoid the Airbnb fees, which are substantial. We have done this before—for several years before Airbnb was even a thing—and can send a rental agreement."

We were all slightly hesitant. Could we really trust these people without a big company being the middleman? Would we be left out in the cold again, but this time—without our money to boot?

I mean, Airbnb has a special note on their site stating, "To protect your payment, never transfer money or communicate outside of the Airbnb website or app." Ohhh boy! What were we in for?

After quite a few more exchanges and a well-drawn-up contract, my sister decided to book the place directly with the owners.

The truth is, we were all uneasy with a lingering feeling of possible doom if they were to change their mind. This was the home that they currently lived in. They told us they were going out of town during that week but what could prevent them from changing their mind?

Meanwhile, since this new STR only had four bedrooms, we realized we would need a second smaller Airbnb to house my oldest sister and her spouse.

So once again, we all went to work scouring the travel portals for what leftovers were available at this short notice. Luckily, we found a unit available at a reasonable price, so we booked it right away. Unfortunately, this was the place I'll tell you about in Chapter 9; I'll give you a hint, it was not a bed of roses for them!

But alas, it was time to fly to Stanford. With bated breath, we arrived group by group to find the second house that we had booked.

Thank goodness, the keys worked, the owners had vacated, and the home was actually really lovely. Not only that, but the owners had also left us a bottle of champagne and a large basket full of wonderful munchies that we consumed immediately because we were all famished from traveling.

As we've discussed in previous chapters, it is sometimes difficult to stay in someone's house who lives in it full time.

But in this case, it wasn't bad at all.

They cleared out space in each closet and cleared out ample drawer space for us as well.

The kitchen was fully stocked, and they told us to eat whatever we wanted. But as good guests do, we just used some of their staples but felt funny diving into their food stash.

The kitchen setup was wonderful and open, which made it easy to entertain our small groups of grads and their families throughout the week.

My husband was thrilled to find a commercial-like coffee/cappuccino maker with a built-in grinder. In fact, he was so enthralled with it that he purchased one for us as soon as we returned home.

Their bedrooms were adequate size though I do have two critiques…

The first is that the bed my husband and I slept in was a trundle bed pulled out to form a queen-sized bed. This posed two problems. You could feel a gap in the middle of the bed where the two mattresses came together. Not a huge issue unless you like to cuddle. Then notoriously, one person or the other falls into the gap, and the mattresses move further apart.

The second complaint is that they had uncomfortable pillows throughout the house. None of us could find one that we liked. They were too lumpy, as if it was filled with chunks of Styrofoam, so your head fell through to the bed, or they were feather pillows that aggravated my allergies.

But enough complaining. Let's get back to the good points of this property.

Although the bathroom that my husband and I shared was small, they provided a basket on the back of the toilet with rolled-up white washcloths. It also included brown washcloths with a note on top requesting for guests to use those to remove makeup so as not to stain the white washcloths permanently. Brilliant!

They had an additional larger basket under the sink, which provided extra towels and a reserve of various bottles of soaps and shampoos. Beside the toilet was a freestanding toilet paper holder for easy access to additional rolls of toilet paper when needed.

One morning, as my husband and I were enjoying our breakfast while the rest of our family was asleep, we admired the view of the backyard and deck through the multitude of sliding glass doors. To our surprise, we noticed a large rat running across the deck. Within minutes, another rat appeared and then another one. It seemed to be a family of them.

We were trying to figure out why they were on the deck and realized they were living underneath the deck. Yuck!

Fortunately, they only seemed to come out at dawn and never bothered us as we relaxed in the sun during the day.

The host also provided a barbeque grill for us on the deck, but thankfully, those rats didn't come out to explore the delicious smells as our steak and chicken cooked to perfection.

In fact, since the rats did not appear during the daylight hours, my family did not even believe our story until we showed them the photos we had taken earlier that day.

Aside from the rats and the minor bedding issues we encountered, this home was very comfortable, and the hosts were wonderful. They had a House Manual that gave us useful information along the way, including how to separate the trash from the recyclables and the composting bin. This was very useful for those of us not from California who are not used to composting.

It was requested that we take the trash to the street for pickup. But this was expected, as we were there for a week and collected quite a bit of trash during our stay.

My oldest sister and her spouse spent all their time hanging out at our house and only used their STR to sleep and shower. So, it turned out to be a joyful week of celebrating my nieces' victory.

As we said goodbye to this beautiful California college town, I wondered if I would ever be back again.

REVIEW: 5 out of 5 stars—although this was no longer pertinent since it was a direct booking and the property did not have a website, no reviews were left

KEY TAKEAWAYS AND DESIGN HOT TIPS

1. Using the various OTAs (Online Travel Agencies) or platforms such as Airbnb, VRBO and Booking.com is understandable. But consider what may happen if they go offline or if you are tagged and banned from these sites.

    The OTA's are a great tool but not your end-all, be-all. I advise you not to rely on them solely for your bookings. You're at the mercy of their guidelines and giving them all your power. You've heard the saying, "Don't put all your eggs in one basket." Well, that applies here as well.

Consider implementing a direct booking site for guests. By creating your own direct-booking site, you can grow your business on your terms. It's time to own your digital real estate, in addition to utilizing the OTAs.

2. Do not use a trundle bed with heavy wooden arms as one of your advertised queen-sized beds. To me, it's as bad as cramming as many "heads in beds" as possible and sleeping in a bunk bed or on an air mattress.

3. I've mentioned this in prior chapters, but it is worth repeating, provide a good variety of thicknesses and firmnesses of pillows for your guests to sleep on.

4. Be aware of rodent or insect issues and hire an exterminator if the problem persists.

THE 5-STAR HOST'R WAY—DIVERSIFYING OTAs

You're halfway through this book, and hopefully, you've seen why it is important to be TIG-centric and become a 5-Star Host'r.

But, can I be frank here?

It's time for a mindset change.

If you are unaware, the Internet game has changed, and we are in a new era.

What worked in the last few years no longer works today. People are taking a different approach to the Internet altogether.

You may have heard murmurs of the "Web 3.0 era," or maybe it's a new term to you. But in either case, it's coming in full force, and it's time to take note and prepare for the third era of the Internet.

The web 3.0 era includes terms like blockchain, cryptocurrency, AI, NFTs, zero-party traffic and so forth. If you're wondering what an NFT is and what all of these new Web 3.0 terms have to do with your business, then you're not alone.

I know this must sound like Greek to many of you; it certainly did to me initially. But I have been studying it fervently to grasp what's happening.

There is too much to cover in this lesson but stay tuned; I will offer more in-depth training on this topic as things develop in the near future.

But for now, I'm going to give you the Cliff Notes version of where it all began and what this new era means for you. Stick with me here!

Web 1.0

The Internet's early era was all about making information accessible to everyone. Web 1.0 delivered on that promise by replacing encyclopedias, phone books, and even library card catalogs. This era was considered "decentralization" from libraries and encyclopedias to an era where everyone could create a website on whatever topic they wanted.

Web 2.0

Then a decade or two later, the web became "centralized" when a handful of major players started to come to the forefront and drew in the majority of the traffic online. The big aggregators came in and consolidated everything. Most online traffic was now going to Google, Apple, Facebook and Amazon for everything. These companies built walls around their technologies and monetized the heck out of them, either through paid services or advertising.

Web 3.0

Then about seven years ago, Web 3.0 spawned from a major data breach of a huge bank where personal accounts were released online. That generated a more frequent occurrence of cyber data breaches, and people started questioning the safety of online banking and purchases. These events caused people to realize that what had become online "centralization" needed to switch back to "decentralization" again.

People began to recognize that some of the power needed to be taken away from the big tech aggregates and returned to the users.

Blockchain was introduced in October 2008. Blockchain provides a system for recording information in a way that makes it difficult or impossible to change, hack, or cheat the system. The goal of Blockchain is to allow digital information to be distributed and recorded but not edited.

Then, **cryptocurrency** was founded—Bitcoin, Ethereum, and the like—a virtual currency system for issuing currency, transferring ownership, and confirming transactions. Rather than being issued by a central authority, it is decentralized.

As this new currency was coming to fruition, people became aware of privacy and trust online. For instance, have you ever asked, "Is Alexa spying on us?"

Did you ever notice that Google, Facebook and Amazon would suddenly send us an ad for something we had just looked at online? It was spooky. It was as if our every move was tracked; in fact, our moves were tracked by cookies and ad-tracking pixels!

Concerns were raised as the general public proclaimed that they did not want Google and Facebook tracking them around the Internet anymore. People wanted a way to take back their privacy and their data.

Apple took note of this and was at the forefront of what came next.

iOS 14.5 Update

In the spring of 2021, Apple took "Privacy" on as its new USP brand. They came out with iOS 14.5, giving end users the choice to opt-out of third-party tracking.

So, at the device level, people could say either, "Yes, I want my information tracked by third-party websites," or "No, I do not." Did you opt-out?

Essentially, this update allowed iPhone users the option to opt-out of having their personal information shared with companies like Facebook, where marketers could no longer rely on ad-tracking pixels for data collection and optimization.

Apple put the power back in the users' hands, and would you believe that 88 percent opted out of tracking in their device?

What did this mean?

Suddenly, Facebook's entire business model of its advertisers relying on off-channel user behavior disappeared. Overnight, what worked for all digital marketing online got shut down and no longer worked.

Facebook took the biggest loss of market share, because of its dependence on third-party data. It literally cut Facebook off at the knees. The old Facebook pixel was now gone, so highly targeted users and traffic sources vanished overnight.

Data could no longer be aggregated, so Facebook lost that ability altogether. Retargeted ads disappeared. Custom audiences no longer exist that worked so well just one year ago.

But it didn't only affect Facebook; it affected businesses, both large and small, who relied on Facebook advertising to gain clients. Effects of this new iOS system led to a 300 percent increase in cost per lead in the first thirty days of its release. That's huge!!

Single channel businesses that were only marketing on Facebook went out of business because they solely depended on that one marketing stream to generate leads. They did not know how to respond and folded.

It was a light switch moment with a ripple effect.

In fact, businesses are still feeling the ripple effect of features that are just no longer available.

But Apple did not stop there…

iOS 15 Update

Six months later, Apple released iOS 15, which was all about mail privacy protection. This meant that advertisers no longer could track the open rates of the emails they sent out.

The new wave is "zero-party data," which means the consumer *willingly* gives us their contact information. In other words, it's now asking and not spying. Zero-party data is explicit data, as the user clearly understands that they voluntarily give you personally identifiable information about themselves.

But if this wasn't enough, Google Analytics—first-party data—is now banned in certain countries. Google Analytics sits behind the scenes and tracks a user's behavior—and this behavior goes beyond what the user clicks on but also tracks and reports on how they scroll, hover, and dwell.

The idea behind all of web 3.0 is for the individual to be able to get control over what's happening. Additionally, any company must now have a purpose to collect and use the data.

Cookies

The use of "cookies" meant the big aggregators collected all sorts of information on us behind the scenes without us even knowing it.

The most common example of this is the flashlight app. Were you aware that when you turned on the flashlight app on your iPhone, it grabbed all your contacts from your phone without you knowing it and without your permission? This caused huge distrust.

Whereas now, we are in a cookieless era. We must willingly accept cookies if they are on a site.

Privacy

Furthermore, privacy will become an even more important topic as time goes on, and privacy policies will be on the front end of a site.

Where Do We Stand Today?

The world has shifted in the last twelve months to a world of distrust. No industry has gone unharmed.

Everywhere you turn, you don't know who to trust, which is causing people to retreat. Then overlay the pandemic, quarantining and inflation on top of that, which is pushing the retreat even further.

Big brands are fundamentally changing their business operations because of what we're seeing. History is repeating itself back to decentralization.

Things are changing at such a rapid pace. It's evolving as we speak.

Going forward, we need to be aware of staying on top of the changes and devise a plan with a different approach.

But it's important to understand that we are at the infancy stage of Web 3.0.

In fact, only 16 percent of the world is in cryptocurrency right now, and only 1 percent are in NFTs. Some real estate transactions now allow cryptocurrency for purchases, so it's coming!

It may not be long before we see the title to properties and cars in the form of an NFT.

The truth is, it's a brand new landscape, and we get to be the captain of the ship, the founders.

This is one of those turn-the-corner moments.

Your competitors don't know how to do it. It's like the Internet in 1998; it was so new that people didn't know if it would last!

How Does This Relate to the Travel Industry?

Not only did the big aggregators see their businesses come to a complete halt, but it was also seen in the travel industry.

But this particular halt was spawned by COVID-19.

In March 2020, Airbnb notified all guests and hosts, despite their cancellation policy, that they could cancel bookings without cause or fee. Hosts had *no* warning of this at all. It shut some people's businesses down for good.

Now, of course, one cannot predict a pandemic, but the point is—there was no warning that Apple was going to turn marketing techniques upside down overnight!

PRICE GOUGING WITH A TWIST

If Apple has the power to do this, don't you think the OTAs do as well?

The Lesson Here:

You never know when something will change online that has a drastic ripple effect sending businesses crashing down. This is a forewarning of what could come and tells us that we should no longer rely solely on these major platforms to serve up qualified leads.

Therefore, OTAs like Airbnb, VRBO and HomeAway.com should not be your be-all-end-all. They can still be a channel for a source of business, but you need to protect yourself by adding a direct-booking site to your toolbelt and start collecting email addresses of your past and future guests.

If you only advertise your listing on the OTAs, you are relying 100 percent on their choices for the lifeblood of your business. Instead, by adding your own direct-booking website to your repertoire, you become 100 percent in control of your own bookings and guest relations.

Consider These Possibilities:

1. Your account can't get hacked and, in turn, shut down if you have your own direct-booking site
2. If you receive several poor reviews in a row on an OTA, you have a hard time getting back on page one of the OTA search
3. The OTAs have the power to shut you down at any time, for any reason
4. If you aren't building a database of past and potential guests, how will you contact them if you get blackballed from the OTA portals?

This is what happens when you put all your eggs in one basket. You have no power. If, instead, you had direct bookings when

COVID-19 hit, you could have at least had the power to pick up the phone and discuss different options with your guest.

Additionally, the OTAs have continual shifts in their operating systems, and their algorithms have gotten so sophisticated that it's hard to keep up.

Hosts can no longer perform all the past proven techniques to securing a first-page listing on an OTA. Things are too complicated now.

Alert! Alert!

If you rely on OTA's to bring you all of your business, you are risking your future success!

The rug can be pulled out from under you as we've seen this happen overnight to many businesses, some of which are giant! They lost 100 percent of their lead flow and client base because they didn't have a backup strategy.

The business market is changing rapidly. Are you paying attention?

Now is your chance to jump ahead of your competitors and start diversifying.

Don't let your competitors climb to the top before you do. Take action with the following steps and scale your business to new heights!

Step 1: Start Collecting Emails From Past Guests

If you choose to hold off on building your own direct-booking site, at a minimum, you need to collect emails from past guests.

Why?

I'm sure you are well aware that when a guest books your property through an OTA, you only receive their telephone number and *not* their email address. The guest's contact info remains the *property of the OTA*. Therefore, you need to find your own way to gather your guest's email addresses when they book your property so you can keep in contact with them about future bookings and referrals.

PRICE GOUGING WITH A TWIST

Email remains the cornerstone of every business out there. It's the most powerful and cost-effective way to build a list of guests. Having your own email list will provide you with a pool of repeat-guests and referrals, which is always a quicker and more reliable way to get consistent bookings than by relying on first-time guests to find your STR out of the masses.

Here are several ways to accomplish that while still utilizing the OTAs for bookings:

- In the check-out letter you send through the OTA, request your guest's email so that you can offer them discounts in the future—analogous to hotel reward points.

- Include a comment card in your property for them to fill out with any improvements they would recommend and also request their email address. Then, you can thank them for helping you out by offering a discount or upgrade to their stay next time, such as a paid dinner or Starbucks card.

- Implement property management software (PMS). This way, you can be listed on Airbnb, VRBO and HomeAway.com simultaneously and not get double booked because the software sorts the dates out. And you can also get direct bookings through this type of software. Some versions are free to $20 a month, and it scales from there, depending on how many properties you have.

- Although OTA's do not share guest email addresses with hosts, they do provide you with the guest's phone number. Why not call them to thank them for their visit and ask if they know anyone looking for a place to stay that is coming to the area?

- Leave a note in your House Manual asking for referrals.

These steps are an excellent start to reducing your over-reliance on OTAs.

Step 2: Build Your Brand and Own Your Traffic

Many hosts complain about the drawbacks of OTAs, but few do anything about it. Most don't even know where to begin.

What are you doing to bring in your own bookings?

If your answer is "nothing," then I want you to think about how hotels drum up new business and follow their lead. Hotels market their brand and services to the people they cater to, and you should do the same.

Think of all the people needing temporary housing in your area.

Here are a few ideas to get you started:

1. Contact local human resources departments—people are always relocating for work and may need temporary housing solutions
2. Set up a Google alert to find new projects or renovations in your area and reach out, offering your STR for them to stay in
3. Contact divorce attorneys—typically, one spouse will move out and may need a place to stay while securing their new permanent housing
4. Contact academic advisors—inquire about visiting professors or students who may need temporary housing for a semester
5. Contact charter airlines—flight crews tire of hotels and may prefer to stay in an STR for their layovers; they could become repeat guests as well
6. Contact performance touring shows—casts often need a place to stay
7. Contact real estate agents—buyers who relocate before they have secured a house and sellers waiting

PRICE GOUGING WITH A TWIST

for a new home to be built may both need temporary housing

8. Contact insurance companies and offer temporary housing solutions for people displaced from their homes due to fire or other natural disasters
9. Get a hub of local businesses to contact—think about who could help or reciprocate services
10. Reach out to past guests—if they had a good experience, they might likely return
11. Ask everyone you know for referrals—offer an Amazon gift card as a thank you

If *you* are not promoting your property, no one else will do it for you.

Step 3: Build Your Own Direct Booking Site

In 2017, OTAs were on the rise. Then, COVID-19 hit in March 2020, and people's businesses came to a screeching halt. This was a warning to hosts that you can't always rely on the OTA platforms.

Many hosts realized that it was okay to continue to leverage OTAs as a tool in their wheelhouse but concluded that they no longer wanted to be shackled by OTAs.

After all, the OTAs own *your* guest's emails and contact information, just as Mark Zuckerberg owns social media. There had to be a way to counteract this and get your stake in the game, and in fact, direct booking websites where guests can book directly with you are your way in. It's the future of hosting.

If you haven't done so already, it's time to branch out and take control of your hospitality business. It's essential, and it's quite simple to do.

What benefits does a direct-booking site offer?

1. Direct booking offers more control over communication with your guests and spurs repeat guests.

2. Repeat guests have the trust factor built-in for both the host and the guest.
3. Direct booking allows both parties to bypass the fees of the OTAs , which leads to more savings.
4. OTA fees will probably increase in the future, and even a small percentage increase in OTA fees will directly affect your bottom line.
5. Being an early adopter grants you access to shift your industry's market to your side and leave your competitors behind you!

Direct booking is, by far, the best way to prepare yourself for web 3.0 and the coming shifts. In an ever-competitive marketplace and a new Internet era, it will be the new standard. Reclaim your freedom from the OTAs and be prepared for the future.

By now, you must be wondering how hard this will be, how much time it will take, and what it will cost. Not to mention, how will you get traffic to your site?

Let me start by saying that your direct-booking site does not have to be anything fancy. In fact, it can be as simple as a one-page site. The price is very reasonable—as of this writing, you can get a site on Squarespace for $12 per month with an annual subscription or $16 month-to-month.

But to make it even easier for you, I've created ready-to-use STR templates that you can find at DiBSTR.com. Just customize them with my step-by-step instructions. It is so intuitive that you could have your site built in a matter of hours.

I also want to point out that you will not get organic traffic from a Google search. In other words, guests will not typically find you through a Google search. Instead, implement these simple steps to gain control over your booking process:

1. Give your property a descriptive, memorable name
2. Customize your Airbnb listing URL to: Airbnb.com/h/yourpropertyname

PRICE GOUGING WITH A TWIST

3. Put a link in your OTA bio that leads to your direct booking website—yes, you can get traffic from the OTAs and drive them to your direct-booking site if they want to see more photos, for example

4. Purchase the domain name for your site—this should be: yourpropertyname.com; the domain name can be purchased from godaddy.com or any host you choose to build your site on, and the average cost is $15-20 per year to own that domain

5. Build a simple one-page website on SquareSpace, Weebly, Wix or WordPress. Or better yet, save yourself the headache and get one of my pre-made templates at **DiBSTR.com** and simply customize it

6. Add your listing, photos, and bio to your site

7. Add a "book now" button—this could link to your favorite OTA, or it can go to your property management system, which acts as an OTA and books for you

8. On your website, give away a freebie in exchange for their email; offer them something they want to be a part of or hot-tips on your locale

9. Consider adding a page or a part of your website dedicated to your TIG, such as corporate travel and business partners or concierge services for business partners; highlight guest satisfaction

10. Display reviews on your website to give potential guests more confidence in booking with you and reduces doubts

Step 4: Email Campaign Strategy

No matter if you follow all three previous steps or only one of them, by now, you understand the importance of collecting emails from every single guest. What you may not know is that you have options of where you can store this information and that you can send out automated emails—like updating past guests about a remodel or new amenities you offer.

In order to do this, you will want to pick an email marketing automation tool like MailChimp or GetResponse. Once your account is set up, you can transfer over your current email list in a CSV format.

Note: As of this writing, MailChimp is free to use for up to 2,000 different emails.

Next, you'll want to set up an automated email marketing "drip" campaign, a specific series of emails sent automatically over time.

Here is an example of an email drip campaign you can follow:

- Welcome email
- Thank you email with a promo code for their next stay
- For the off-season or lower occupancy months, send an email saying, "We just opened up reservations for (time period), but spots are going quickly, so book now."
- Update them on what's going on in your area—remember that they want to live like a local, so become the local Grand Ambassador for your place; build a sample itinerary and offer discount codes.
- Thirty days later, send an email asking if they're looking to travel again and provide a link to your direct-booking site.

The key is sending emails with content that people care about, so they open them and read them.

Bottom line: If you're not doing this, you are getting beat by the hosts who are.

Step 5: Brand and Collect Emails Through Wi-Fi

Our final step to gathering emails is quite ingenious.

Did you know that you can actually install a Wi-Fi device that allows you to brand your Wi-Fi for your guests?

Let me explain...

If you have recently stayed at a hotel, you are aware that when you arrive as their guest, you are prompted to log into their customized page—called a "splash page." Once you have given them your name and email and accepted their terms, you can use their Internet service at no fee.

These Wi-Fi systems are sophisticated and expensive and would not make sense for the STR host to install. However, a "Wi-Fi Access Point" device gives the STR owner a similar type of access for a very minimal cost.

This device plugs into your existing router, so it broadcasts a separate "Guest Wi-Fi" in the home. In other words, you can keep everything running on your old Wi-Fi network, like the TVs and anything else you set up on that Wi-Fi, so there is no need to rewire everything in the home.

These devices are so simple to install that it only takes five minutes to set up, and they work with any Internet provider/ISP. Once plugged in, you can customize your splash page background to anything you want, such as a photo of your property or the area.

As soon as your guest turns on their computer, this branded page will appear. Then, they simply agree to your terms and fill in their name and email under Guest Wi-Fi and voila—they are online, and now you have their email and a way to contact them in the future—all while providing a better Wi-Fi experience for your guests.

The contact information can integrate directly with your email service provider—like MailChimp or GetResponse, as mentioned in Step 4—and allows you to take control of your guest data while ensuring guests remember your brand, not Airbnb or VRBO.

Finally, as previously mentioned, getting page-one presence on Google will be hard at the beginning, so that is not a reliable strategy. Fortunately, the number one source to get direct bookings is from previous guests, and this system offers that up on a silver platter.

Once you automate your marketing to your previous guests, you will start generating more direct bookings and gathering those coveted 5-star reviews.

It's time to take your power back. He who has the data will win.

Changes, they are a coming! Are you ready?

5-STAR HOST'R ACTION PLAN

1. Follow the design hot tips
2. Implement systems to collect email addresses from your guests
3. Implement strategies to gain your own guest traffic
4. Build your own direct booking website by customizing one of my pre-made STR templates found at: DiBSTR.com
5. Implement an email drip campaign
6. Purchase a Wi-Fi device to collect guest emails at: https://stayfi.com?lmref=roYiVA

SECTION 3
Renting Small Spaces

If you are an STR Host renting out small spaces, this comes with its own challenges.

In some cases, you may be renting out a room in your house while you live there too. You may have a space separate from your home yet connected or separate living space on your property, such as a carriage house in your backyard.

Each of these scenarios will be discussed in this section.

As in the past sections, no matter where you are in your journey, make sure to follow my Key Takeaways at the end of each chapter to avoid many common mistakes and make sure to really absorb the information in "5-Star Host'r Way" section and implement what serves you in your business to sustain a steady stream of 5-star reviews.

Chapter 8

MAYHEM IN MILAN

It was my niece's college junior year abroad in Spain, and she had a holiday weekend coming up. So, she and her friend decided to take a short trip to Milan, Italy.

All her life, she had observed her mother scouring through Airbnbs to find perfect vacation locations. Being on a limited budget, my niece decided to take this route as well. So, she began her search for an "entire apartment" and found just the right one.

To their surprise, once they arrived, they found their rental was actually one room within a small apartment. Not good. This should have been advertised as a "private room" and not as an "entire place." That's a very big difference! Can you say "false advertising?"

Can you imagine how surprised you would be to open the front door and find a woman already living there? That's what happened to these two young ladies.

I mean, what do you say? Especially when you are in a foreign country and don't speak their language!

They soon found out that the owner spoke some broken English because she asked to see their passports. Apparently, in Europe, they insist on meeting you and checking your passport to make sure you are who you say you are. Fair enough!

But they were left wondering what the heck had gone wrong. Had this woman made a mistake, or did she intentionally mislead them?

In either case, this was the situation that they found themselves in, and they realized that they would have to make the best of it.

The setup was as follows:

The owner lived on one side of the apartment, and the guests had a bedroom on the other side. There was only one bathroom, and it was off the hallway. It wasn't connected to the bedroom that they were in, so they had to share it with the owner. Awkward!

Sidenote: The owner did not provide any toiletries or amenities to make the girls' stay more enjoyable, but fortunately, they had packed the needed essentials.

Here's how my niece described the layout, "So the owner could come into our bathroom or could come into our bedroom, but both could be locked. There was a hallway between them, but she just stayed on her side of the apartment. And we were on the other side of the apartment, and there was kind of like a screen, like one of those dividers to divide two areas, but you could see through it. Like, I could still see what she was doing, and she could probably see over the screen to watch us."

They also shared a very small kitchen with the owner. Fortunately, they were eager to try the local Italian cuisine, so they ate most of their meals out.

The second issue with this "private room" is that the owner had a very large dog, and the dog was not contained to the owner's side of the apartment. The dog frequently wandered over to visit my niece and her friend, even though he wasn't summoned.

And you guessed it, the owner did not advertise or mention that there was a dog or any type of pet living in the place.

The day my niece and her friend were leaving, the owner had already left to go to work for the day. They were packed up and all set to check-out at 10 am. The owner had instructed to simply shut the door behind them and told them that it locked automatically.

Okay, so she wasn't in her apartment when they were leaving, but guess who was?

Yep, the dog was. And it was a huge dog. And he started growling and barking at them. And my niece's friend was really terrified of dogs and didn't want to leave the room with the dog being there. The dog was literally blocking the path to the front door of this place, so they were trapped by the dog.

My niece knew they had to get out of there soon because they had a train to catch. So, she texted the owner to ask her how to address the dog situation. Finally, one of her neighbors came over, grabbed the dog, and saved the day. Phew!

Off they went on their travels!

Sadly, right after they returned to Spain from their Milan trip, COVID-19 hit. You all know this story—they were preparing to shut the borders, so my niece had to find a flight within twenty-four hours and return to the USA immediately. Then, she had twenty-four hours to find temporary housing for a ten-week period because the Stanford campus had closed and everything went online. But alas, it all worked out!

REVIEW: 4 out of 5 stars

They ended up giving 4 out of 5 stars because they did complain to Airbnb about being misled on sharing a home versus renting the entire home, as well as the presence of the dog. Luckily, they did get a partial refund from Airbnb—something like 50 percent.

KEY TAKEAWAYS AND DESIGN HOT TIPS

1. When listing your property on any STR platform, list it in the proper category. A "private room" means sharing the living space with the owner.

2. If you are renting a shared space, mention any pets in the home. Many people have allergies to animals and could not stay there.

3. Even if you are renting out a room in a house in which you currently live, provide travel-sized toiletries and whatever else your TIG will need during their stay.

THE 5-STAR HOST'R WAY—ELEVATED GUEST EXPERIENCE

It is of utmost importance to realize that once you decide to open your house to paying guests, you need to focus on making a good impression. Running an STR is not like inviting guests over for a weekend to crash in your spare bedroom. It's a serious business that requires planning, time, and effort. A poor impression will leave your guests with a bad taste in their mouths and, in turn, lead to less than stellar reviews.

So how do you go about renting a small space the right way?

Think of how well-known hotels operate and cater to their guests and follow their lead. Hotels provide an elevated guest experience, and you need to do the same.

Hotels offer concierge services, bars and restaurants, workout facilities, and so on. Each area is designed specifically to meet the guests' needs.

Now envision the design of the guest rooms and bathrooms. Picture the toiletries and the selection in the coffee bar and food prep areas. Every single item they offer was chosen with their ideal guest in mind.

Therefore, think of your place as a hotel and consider the TIG you are catering to. Great hosts meet unrecognized needs. They anticipate what a guest will need before the guest is even aware they need it.

Picture this as weaving a web to entice your TIG and encourage them to stay.

First, gauge why they're choosing your location and your particular property. Also, realize that hotels afford you the fantasy of what you don't have at home while providing the comforts of home. You need to match or top this.

You're in the hospitality business when you run an STR. Therefore, your guests are paying good money to receive a service they feel they deserve. Realize that part of providing hospitality is to make your guests feel special and appreciated.

Think through what you would like if you were a visiting guest. Ask yourself, *what would I want in that situation?* Make each service about them and not you.

Most importantly, remember that it's not transactional; it's relationship-based. It's important to make your guests feel at home as if they were your family. Do whatever it takes to elevate their experience while they are there.

Here are some suggestions for an elevated guest experience. These tips apply whether you rent a whole house or a room in a shared home:

1. Leave a Personalized Welcome Note

Add a personal touch by leaving a handwritten note welcoming them to your home. Make sure to write their name on it as this makes them feel more special.

2. Personalize Their Stay

Get to know your guests ahead of time and provide personalized goodies. You can do this by putting together a short questionnaire to send your guest right after they book your property asking what types of food they like and what their interests and hobbies are.

For instance, if they say they like yoga, provide a yoga mat or let them know where the nearest yoga studio is. The same goes for telling a runner where the running path is or the vegan where the closest vegan restaurants are.

This process takes about thirty to forty-five minutes per guest but is so worth the extra time and effort.

3. Give Them a Small Gift Upon Arrival

Ask why they're coming to town and give them a bottle of champagne if it's their anniversary. This produces elevated reciprocity.

4. Provide a Welcome Basket

A welcome basket is a surefire way to make a guest smile during check-in.

Consider providing a locally sourced welcome basket to create a moment of delight upon their check-in, or fill the basket with personalized goodies they like.

5. Provide Additional Amenities

Think about what your guests may want and need during their stay and provide it for them.

This includes toiletries. Don't wait for them to call asking where the extra toilet paper is. Be prepared with more than what you think they may need. All guests will appreciate this.

Be anticipatory of what extras they might need. For instance, it's nice to include extra earbuds, and cell phone chargers in case guests forgot theirs.

Consider the following categories: hunger, thirst, rest, and comfort.

Here are some other items to consider:

- Equipment they may need during their stay, climate and location dependent
- Keep items like a booster seat or baby wipes, if you run a family-friendly STR
- Tea/hot chocolate/coffee maker
- First aid kit with Motrin and Tylenol
- Extension cords
- Hair dryer and an iron or steamer

6. Think of What They May Have Forgotten

Spoil them even more with a basket full of items they may have forgotten to pack.

Include items such as the following:
- Toothbrush and toothpaste
- Q-tips
- Cotton balls
- Makeup removing cloths
- Sunscreen
- Advil

Leave a note letting them know this is for their use. Design something like this on canva.com:

For Our Guests
ENJOY YOUR STAY

Please Help Yourselves
USE WHAT YOU NEED
&
LEAVE THE REST FOR ANOTHER GUEST

7. Make Your Offerings More Experiential

It's the details that make the stay just a little more special. Think of something a guest wants but doesn't know is available to them. For example, you could create a guide highlighting the best places to eat out and visit in the neighborhood.

Think of how you can enrich the lives of your guests and create value for them. This is the greatest determinant of your success.

Surprise and delight travelers with things like:

- Offer candlelight dinner that's catered in
- If sharing your space, offer to cook dinner for them
- A warm drink or wine when they arrive

8. Provide a Thank You Card

Provide a handwritten card on their way out thanking them for visiting and inviting them to stay at your place again on their next visit to town.

9. Cultivate Repeat Visitors

Become a guest relationship specialist and connect with your guest for repeat stays and referrals. Make sure to note their personal preferences to impress them when they return.

- Pay attention to the snacks they eat and what they like and have it available for them for their next visit
- Set up a massage for them
- Leave a handwritten card that says thank you again for booking and leave a Starbucks gift card

Do not underestimate the lifetime value of guests.

5-STAR HOST'R ACTION PLAN

1. Create a questionnaire to send guests before they arrive and personalize their stay.
2. Decide what you will put in your welcome basket and forgot basket and purchase the needed items.
3. Brainstorm ideas of what can elevate your guest's experience.

Chapter 9

SENSORY OVERWHELM

During the same summer trip to California to attend my twin nieces' graduation from Stanford, my sister and her spouse rented an Airbnb that couldn't be described any other way than "sensory overwhelm."

Let me explain.

It was our second day of vacation, and we were expecting my sister and her spouse to come to the "big house" our family had rented to join us for a tasty breakfast.

As soon as they entered our home, we knew something was wrong. My poor sister was covered in hives.

"What happened?" we gasped.

Well—unfortunately, their night had not gone so well.

Somberly, she began to tell us about one of the worst night's sleep of her life.

They had arrived at their STR to what appeared to be a very nice and well-planned carriage house below the owner's house. When they settled in for the night, they thought, *this place is really quaint*.

Unfortunately, that feeling of comfort did not last long.

As soon as they pulled the covers back and crawled into bed, they knew something was off. Any little movement caused a crackly sound, and boy was it uncomfortable. They pulled back the fitted sheet to find a waterproof vinyl mattress cover.

Had a previous guest soiled the bed, they wondered? Why else would an STR host put such an uncomfortable item on the bed? Not to mention how it produced sweating in a hot climate, ugh!

So, they begrudgingly got up to undo the whole bed to remove the vinyl covering and then remade the bed.

They breathed a sigh of relief and looked forward to a good night's sleep.

As they settled in under the covers for the second time that night, they were rudely awakened by the owners' TV blaring in the unit above them. They looked at the clock, and it was 11:00 pm. *Okay,* they thought, *we will give it until midnight to quiet down.*

My sister said, "I think they must have hardwood floors with no insulation because when the TV plays, it sort of reverberates, and I can hear this deep male voice, and I think it must be the guy that lives there. So I finally put my earplugs in, and I could still hear it through that."

As the minutes slowly ticked by, they turned into hours. Sadly, it was 2:00 am before the owners turned their TV off and went to bed.

"At last," my sister thought, "now we can get some much-needed sleep."

So, they closed their eyes and then realized the owners left their front porch light on; it was blasting through their window. "It felt like it was like midday," they exclaimed.

Oh dear, this did not sound good! At this point, they were starting to get sensory overwhelm and simply could not fall asleep.

At some point in the wee hours, they dozed off for a brief period, but my sister woke up because she felt itchy all over.

Apparently, the owners had washed the sheets in a highly scented laundry detergent, and my sister broke out in hives in the middle of the night. She took the sheets off the bed and wrapped up in the blanket trying to sleep that way for the remaining hours.

SENSORY OVERWHELM

Of course, this led to her having to run out the first thing that morning to buy unscented laundry detergent before they even came to see us. She said, "so now when we return, I'll have to wash them and re-make the bed."

What a way to start a vacation, huh?

Every one of her senses was on overload. Even Benadryl wasn't calming down her hives, but she was a trooper and persevered.

So later that day, they asked if I would come over and critique their Airbnb, as I had before in Lawrence.

As soon as we walked in, I smelled something very odd. As I looked around, I found two things causing this horrible aroma.

The first one was the cleaning solution used in the kitchen area. The countertops were putting off this horribly strong, unpleasant chemical odor.

Then, I noticed several Glade PlugIns—probably there to mask the cleaning solution odor. As I looked further, I noticed every room contained a Glade PlugIn. They were giving off a very off-putting and perfumy scent. In fact, it soon made me nauseous. I suggested that we unplug them and put them away in a cupboard where they wouldn't affect my sister's sensitive hive condition.

When inspecting the bedroom, I noticed that atop the bench at the foot of the bed lay a chest with a beautiful African hand-carved chess set on it. Although it was very pretty and decorative, I asked them, "is that in your way?"

They chuckled and said, "you don't know how many times we have already knocked into that and chess pieces fell off. Not to mention, we could use that space to sit and put on our shoes."

Fortunately, my sister knew how to play chess, so she knew how to set it up again, but I wouldn't have known how. Besides, you risk losing pieces to the game by leaving it set up.

Moving on, I noticed this property had nice parquet hardwood floors in the main living space, but the bedroom had wall-to-wall carpet. Both areas had many small throw rugs that were more of a bother than anything. The ones on the hardwood floor were constantly slipping all over the place, which is not very smart from a safety standpoint, especially for older people.

I'm not sure why there were throw rugs in the bedroom since it was carpeted, but I suppose they thought it would protect the carpet? The problem, though, was that the edges were curling up and posed a dangerous trip hazard if you had to get up to go to the bathroom during the night.

What's more, all these rugs would be difficult for a cleaning crew because when you're vacuuming, the fringe always gets caught in the vacuum cleaner and then you have to step on them to get it cleaned. The same holds true if the edges are coming up.

Next, I pointed out that there was no mirror in the bedroom. I think it's important to have a mirror in every bedroom so that you don't have to be in the one bathroom everyone shares when you want to get ready. It frees up space and provides a quick way to primp. I also believe there needs to be one full-length mirror somewhere in the property for your guests to get a quick once-over before heading out.

I reminded them that I preach that anything a hotel has, an STR needs to have, such as hangers, luggage racks, extra blankets, hair dryer, mirrors, and so on.

Finally, I checked out the bathroom and noted limited space to put anything. I suggested that it would be nice to add a shelving unit above the toilet, so you at least had a spot to place a cosmetic bag or Dopp kit. But there wasn't even room for a toothbrush.

I added that it was nice that they provided a shampoo, conditioner, and soap container in the shower. But my sister chimed in, "I always bring my own bottles, so it's nice that at least the top of the container is flat so I can put my bottles there. Otherwise, I'd have no room for that either, and that is always frustrating for me."

Lastly, I observed clothes pins on the draperies. I gasped, "What on earth! That's odd and quite unattractive."

SENSORY OVERWHELM

My sister laughed and said, "I brought those because I need to have it dark, so I've learned to travel with clips to clip the draperies closed. People don't typically think about that, and I always wish hosts would stay a few nights in their place to see what their guest experiences."

She was right, but in this situation, even the clips did not provide the darkening effect she had hoped for because of the bright light outside her window that was left on all night.

I said, "It's good to have the host stay, and it's also good to have someone that the host knows stay who can give good feedback because some people go to bed and wake up at all different times. The host needs to be aware of lighting issues as well as sound issues."

My sister added, "So if you live in the same building as your STR, you have to be aware of your hours and your voices. You know, it's still your house, but you've invited guests that are paying for the right to be there. Right? You can't be staying up till two in the morning talking loudly. It's just unfair. If that happened in a hotel, we would ask to change rooms."

It really wouldn't have taken much for this STR host to make this place more comfortable. As I have mentioned before, it is essential to think like your guest. Put yourself in their shoes and offer what you would want if you paid for the space.

REVIEW: 3 out of 5 stars

They ended up giving a review of 3 out of 5-stars, but here's the funny thing:

The host wrote them afterward, asking where her mattress pad and Glade PlugIns were. Of course, my sister wrote back promptly, telling the owner where they were. It turns out their host was upset because one Glade PlugIn was missing, and she wanted to know why they were removed.

Seriously, why would anyone take those home with them? Especially these stinky ones!

But they kept their tongue and wrote back apologizing if one was missing. They explained that they had put them all away in the cabinet because they don't respond well to chemicals in the air. They also replied that the vinyl mattress pad was very uncomfortable and noisy, so they removed it to be able to sleep.

They never heard back from the host, but one can only hope the host took these things as constructive criticism and put the changes into practice for their next guests.

KEY TAKEAWAYS AND DESIGN HOT TIPS

1. Be aware of outdoor lighting that may affect your guests' sleep at night. This could be anything from porch lights to spotlights to security lights. Even little twinkle lights that hang up along the edge of the window and never go off shine through the window; they're so pretty when viewed from the outside but not so pretty when you're inside trying to sleep. Lights that don't turn off make it difficult to relax as a guest. Provide a way for the guest to turn off any lights that may shine in the windows.

2. Install black-out drapes—that actually meet in the center—in all bedrooms.

3. Ensure that the property is soundproof. If your home connects to the STR property, consider your guests, and keep your voices and TV volume down.

4. Do not use perfumed anything because many people have chemical sensitivities.

5. Do not use vinyl mattress protectors; they are uncomfortable, noisy, and hot. Your STR is not a nursing home.

6. Your best investment is in a comfortable mattress.

    I've stayed in many STRs where the host uses their old mattress, convincing themselves that it was

SENSORY OVERWHELM

adequate for them and deducing their guest is only going to stay there a night or two, so it should be fine. This is unfair to the paying guest and certainly does not warrant a 5-star review.

At a minimum, add a layer of memory foam on top of the mattress. People will notice it. Of course, that's more expensive, but if you want to be at the top and want the best reviews, you've got to pay a little extra.

7. In addition to the comfort of the mattress, high quality, high thread count sheets make a huge difference.

8. Provide plenty of room in the bathroom for your guest's belongings.

9. You might consider taping throw rugs down to the hardwood floor to prevent them from slipping but do a small test area because you risk ruining the finish on your floors.

   The non-slip pads that you lay under the rug are another solution, but those seem to move around as well, and then you always have to move the rug to cover up the unsightly pad. It certainly poses a dilemma, so keep these concerns in mind when furnishing your property with throw rugs. The best solution is to use heavier or bigger rugs to avoid some of these concerns.

10. Avoid decorative items that are droppable, breakable, or have many pieces. Select games and accessories accordingly, and don't overdo it—have a cabinet, drawer, or shelf to store games rather than leave them out as décor. Provide plenty of flat surfaces where guests can place their belongings.

THE 5-STAR HOST'R WAY—CLEANING AND SENSORY TIPS

A paying guest who comes to stay at your STR has chosen your property rather than a hotel. Hence, you need to make sure their experience rivals what they might expect from a hotel. Think about what they receive during a hotel stay and provide the same or better. But above all, make sure your STR is comfortable, in good working order and clean.

The best way to ensure your property is cleaned thoroughly between bookings is to create a consistent cleaning routine that can be easily followed each and every time.

Hiring professional cleaners guarantees your property is cleaned from top to bottom. Find a company specializing in rentals, and they'll pay close attention to areas you might overlook.

It's best if you first know your property's cleaning and turnover procedures before handing it over to a cleaning crew. This way, you can document the steps and provide them with a step-by-step checklist on cleaning the property after every guest.

In addition, take photos showing exactly where furnishings should be placed. It is wise also to take photos of what settings to use on appliances, thermostats, TV and Wi-Fi, and anything else requiring specific instructions.

To achieve those coveted 5-star reviews, your STR must be sparkling clean and tidy.

Remember, every guest should arrive and feel as if they're the first guest ever to step foot inside. It's all about the details.

Commit to higher cleaning standards and ensure your cleaning and turnover crews agree to follow a consistent cleaning routine.

Feel free to use the following cleaning and turnover guide as a template. Get more detailed if you wish, add more pages, and brand it to work for your STR.

By compiling a guide like this for your STR, along with photos, no matter who is turning over your property, they'll know exactly what to do.

Cleaning and Turnover Guide

Property Information

- Property Name:
- Property Address:
- Photo of Property
- Number of Bedrooms:
- Number of Bathrooms:
- Access:
- Parking:
- Wi-Fi:
- Garbage:
- Important Information:

Laundry

Note: Since doing a load of laundry is the most time-consuming task during turnovers, have your cleaning crew collect dirty linens and start the washing machine as soon as they enter the property.

- Gather all dirty linens throughout the property
- Start laundry—see photo for washing machine settings

Dishes

- Load all dishes and start the cycle if that hasn't been done already by the guest

WI-FI

- Connect to the Wi-Fi to make sure it is operating correctly

Overall

- Walk through the property and report any damages or excessive mess to the host
- Note any maintenance issues or missing items and report them to the host
- Report any gifts or thank you cards left behind for the host

Kitchen

- For your safety, make sure to unplug appliances before cleaning
- Toss, donate, or remove any remaining condiments, food, or beverages
- Wipe down hard surfaces, including countertops, tables, sinks, cabinets, and floors, to remove grease, dust, dirt and germs
- Clean cabinet interiors and stage the contents
- Wipe down the outside and inside of the oven
- Wipe down the outside and inside of the refrigerator and freezer, including the top
- Re-stage the refrigerator with bottles of water
- Wipe down the outside and inside of the microwave, including the top

Entire House

- Dust all furniture, including ceiling fan and light fixtures
- Empty all trash bins, place a neatly folded trash bag at the bottom, and then line the bin with another bag
- Sweep, mop, vacuum all floors, throw rugs, carpets
- Refill all liquids, including hand soap, dish soap, bath soaps, olive oil, salt, pepper, etc.

- Replace all consumables like paper towels, sponges, and toilet paper
- Check that bulbs in lamps and light fixtures are working; replace as needed

Dining Room and Eating Area
- Wipe down the table and chairs
- Move chairs to sweep, vacuum, or mop underneath

Living Room
- Vacuum under cushions of chairs and sofas
- Re-stage all pillows, throws, and furniture as you see in the photo—provide photos of staging to your liking
- Check to ensure TV is working and Netflix is still logged in
- Turn heat to 62 and/or AC off
- Check that remote control batteries are working and re-stage in the media console

Bedrooms
- Make beds with clean, stain-free bedding
- Look under beds for items left behind
- Check dresser drawers, clean if necessary
- Stage bed exactly like photo—provide photos of staging to your liking

Bathroom
- Sanitize toilet
- Clean sink
- Clean tub with non-abrasive cleaner
- Open all drawers and cabinets, clean if necessary

- Ensure blow dryer still works
- Re-stock drawers, cabinets, and tub/shower per photos
- Fold toilet paper end into a triangle—add branded sticker, optional
- Re-stage bathroom exactly like photo—provide photos of staging to your liking
- Re-stock and re-stage the Forgot Something basket per photo

Guest Towels

- Leave two bath towels per guest
- Leave one hand towel per guest
- Leave one makeup towel per guest
- Tri-fold and stage just like the photo
- Re-stage a clean, stain-free bath mat

Dishes

- Empty dishwasher

Laundry

- If you haven't already, transfer the wash to the dryer—review photos for settings
- Always clean out the vents and filters before and after every load

Cleaning Supplies

- Dispose of any expired cleaning products
- Refill supplies you've used to assure you are ready for the next turnover

Security

- Re-set Smartlock or confirm keys and lockbox are working properly

- Close and lock all windows and doors before you leave
- Message the host that the property is guest ready

5-STAR HOST'R ACTION PLAN

1. Follow the design hot tips
2. Design your own cleaning and turnover guide along with photos
3. Have friends stay in your space and critique it:

    Have them start from the very beginning with your check-in instructions. Have a checklist with the following:

    - Are your check-in instructions clear?
    - Do your parking directions make sense?
    - Can you find your way to the entrance at night?
    - Is your House Manual helpful and easy to understand?
    - Are your essentials and amenities above average?
    - Is the bed comfortable, and did they find enough selection for pillows?
    - Do you have adequate space to put your luggage and belongings?
    - Is the water pressure sufficient, and are any drains sluggish?
    - Is the check-out process smooth?

    If any hiccups appear along the way, take the time to make the proper adjustments and repairs, make your listing details and House Manual clearer, and fine-tune your check-in and check-out instructions.

4\. Spend a night or two in your own STR:

It's valuable to stay in your space at least once a quarter to analyze it in all seasons. This way, you can see what's needed or what could be improved. Being your own guest can help you find areas for improvement.

Chapter 10

SIMPLE SPLENDOR

And now for the crème de la crème.

As one typically does, I have saved the best for last. Above and beyond all others, this place was our favorite stay. In fact, we loved it so much that we went back for a second time. This is the *only* property we have gone to more than once.

My twin nieces had just started their freshman year at Stanford University, and my husband wanted to start a tradition of visiting them in the fall each year for a football game.

We weren't sure if we would cramp their style, but they enthusiastically encouraged us to come for a visit.

They were eager to show us around and introduce us to the new friends made recently.

My husband found the cutest place on Airbnb in Menlo Park, just minutes from the University.

So, what made this place so great, you ask?

Let me tell you—just about everything.

This property is listed on Airbnb as a "Creekside Serenity," and that's an understatement!

Here's how one guest described it, "It felt like a world away where you are surrounded by the sound of birds singing and the creek nearby."

I believe that is an accurate description. Let me tell you about it.

When we arrived, we parked our car in the allotted spot on the premises. The owner happened to be leaving her home to run some errands. So, we got a chance to meet her face-to-face.

She was lovely and told us not to hesitate to contact her for anything that may come up or with any recommendations we might want from her for places to eat, shop, or the best places to hike.

She guided us to the backyard and pointed to the lovely cottage we would stay in for the next four days.

The host's main house and the carriage house shared a beautiful, serene backyard. But the host left the backyard to us and never once appeared.

It was as if we had our own private house, with the owner right there in case we needed anything.

The pathway up to the carriage house was a beautifully landscaped oasis.

The property had a private entrance with a lockbox for self-check-in.

This particular property was basically a 350-square-foot studio apartment with the bedroom and living space all in one large room. It was definitely compact, but it didn't feel cramped. She cleverly utilized every spare inch of space to the fullest.

Because the place was a studio without a separate bedroom, I would have anticipated a Murphy bed—a bed constructed so that it could be folded down from the wall. Instead, we found a comfortable queen-size bed, yet the space was designed to leave plenty of room for everything else.

In fact, here is all that this place offered:

SIMPLE SPLENDOR

At the front of the room was a small kitchen table up against the wall with two chairs, adequate for dining or working. She had left us a beautiful welcome basket with fresh fruit and healthy snacks as well as various brochures displaying local events that we may find of interest.

She also provided a House Manual listing interesting attractions, local restaurants, and shopping suggestions. It also included instructions on how to use the TV, the Internet, and how to program the thermostat.

Above the kitchen table was a wall-mounted TV with a remote. She offered Netflix, HBO, and all the channels one would want.

The bathroom, though small, was perfectly adequate for us. The sink provided space to lay a few toiletries, shelving in the shower offered a place for our items, and shelving above the toilet stored extra toilet paper, extra towels, and left room for our cosmetic bag and Dopp kit.

She provided all the necessary toiletries as well as a hair dryer.

Beside the queen-size bed was a comfortable reading chair with a side table, and little tables and reading lights flanked both sides of the bed. She even placed chocolates for us on our night tables.

The small kitchenette provided space for guests to cook their own meals, including a two-burner stove top next to a kitchen sink. Above the sink was a double cabinet filled with dinnerware, glassware, cups, and various serving bowls. Below this counter were cleaning supplies and a fire extinguisher.

A small microwave sat above a set of pull-out storage bins filled with utensils and kitchen gadgets. Next to this was a closet twelve to eighteen inches deep with multiple shelves containing all the cooking basics such as pots and pans, a colander, a toaster, a blender, a coffee machine, and various cooking bowls and measuring cups.

Beside this closet was a full-sized refrigerator with a freezer. She was kind enough to leave us fresh, cold bottles of water.

She had literally thought of everything and somehow managed to fit all of this into this quaint little house.

On the wall opposite the bed was an entire set of closets with a bookshelf at the end.

Inside the closet were hangers, an ironing board and an iron, as well as extra pillows, bed sheets, blankets, and towels. The closet had space for dresses as well as many dresser drawers for folded clothes. This was the largest closet space I had seen in an STR, let alone a compact carriage house with limited space.

She had a small outdoor patio set off to the side so we could sip a cup of coffee, while enjoying the tranquil peace. She even had a hammock hanging between her trees for a restful swing.

I mean to tell you, she thought of everything. Every last detail was chosen carefully with the guest's comfort in mind.

REVIEW: 5+ out of 5 stars

We gave her a review of 5 out of 5-stars both times that we stayed there. We would have given her more if that had been an option!

But it wasn't just us—this is how another guest described the host in their review, "The host was helpful, striking a balance between friendliness and giving us privacy."

Another guest said, "It was a perfect setting for a week-long retreat where I needed peace and solitude. The cottage is conveniently located near Stanford, Menlo Park shops and downtown Palo Alto, with access to bike paths and hiking trails. The host was very attentive and communicative. The cottage was sparkling clean and very well appointed with everything you may need to make your stay more comfortable. Special touches were evident throughout."

KEY TAKEAWAYS AND DESIGN HOT TIPS

1. Utilize small spaces to the fullest. Every closet space can be used to the fullest by adding shelves.
2. Follow everything this host did as detailed above.

THE 5-STAR HOST'R WAY—DESIGN AND STYLING

So, for our final lesson, it's time to wrap up everything you have learned thus far with a big beautiful bow—and that bow is "design and styling."

As you well know, the colossal success of OTAs like Airbnb and VRBO has created enormous competition.

Standing out in this crowded industry has become a real challenge. However, one thing stands above all others, to maximize your returns.

Without a doubt, the number one way to get an edge on the competition is through *design*. By elevating your STR with design and styling, you will optimize your listing and ensure that the images posted online really stand out and boost the impression your property makes in order to magnetize guests.

Design Foundation

As discussed throughout this book, knowing your ideal guest is imperative. This knowledge has come to play in many categories, but it is essential when it comes to design because you want to design everything around that person.

Surprisingly, the majority of guidance out there for STR design teaches hosts to focus on having a *broad appeal* to draw in more guests.

But I believe this is completely WRONG! I believe the opposite is true. You should design your furnishings based on your location, the architectural design of your property, and most importantly, on your TIG.

Let's refer to the hotel industry one more time. As you know, hotels have a specific guest type they cater to, and their interior design reflects that.

Each space is designed to focus on making the shell of their space "guest ready."

In fact, most hotels provide a multitude of areas designed for different guest purposes, such as:

- Lobby—the wow factor, what a guest first sees and where they get information and can relax
- Restaurant—where guests eat their meals
- Bar—entertainment and cocktails
- Computer/Meeting Rooms—where work gets done
- Bedrooms—where guests sleep, watch TV and shower
- Ballrooms—area for special gatherings
- Workout facilities—where guests exercise
- Exterior features—pools, lounge areas, outdoor games, etcetera.

Depending on the clientele you serve and the size of your property, allocate space for each of these areas—the last three on the list are optional.

As you can see from the story just told, the host allocated space for almost each of these categories, and that was in a 350 square foot cottage!

No matter if you are renting out a room in your home, leaving your home for someone to stay in while you are gone, or you purchased it specifically to become an STR, that space is no longer just a place for your friends to crash, it's going to be occupied by paying guests.

Therefore, whether you are starting with a blank slate or already have your STR fully furnished and you are looking for an edge, designing your space to suit your TIG is crucial.

By following this rule, you will be able to create memorable spaces that are constantly sought after.

Breaking Down Design Into Bite-Sized Pieces

Designing a room is much more than simply buying new products. Throughout my years of design and staging, I learned the most valuable step was gathering information at the beginning to understand the expectations for the space and the guest.

The process includes identifying the room's problems, understanding the guests' design aesthetic, establishing the budget, and then blending it with my special creative touch.

In its basic form, effective interior design must be considered from two viewpoints: the functional and the visual.

But I have devised a three-step process for creating a unique elevated space.

I call this "**The 3 D's of Design**":

1. Deliberate Design—Functional, start with a plan
2. Desirable Design—Visual, pleasing to look at
3. Distinctive Design—Styling, photo-opp ready

You'll want to follow each of these steps in the order presented. Let's go over each of them.

Step 1: Deliberate Design

Deliberate design is all about the *function* of the space. Function is the foundation of designing a space. It should always be your starting point.

Function is simply what the space or furniture is intended for, its purpose. It's about prioritizing how you will use the room or piece of furniture over how it looks.

The goal is to maximize the function of the space and to create a comfortable area for your TIG.

Here are some tips on how to maximize the function of a space:

1. Purpose of the Room

A functional room utilizes the space for its intended purpose. For example:

- Bedroom = sleeping
- Office = working on a computer
- Kitchen = food prep and consumption
- Living Room = social gatherings, reading a book, or watching TV

If a home is attractive but doesn't function well, it will cause guests to be frustrated and uncomfortable. Therefore, you must design with a purpose.

For each room, you need to define the most efficient use of that space. Ask yourself, "What is this space used for? What is its purpose?"

In the case of a small space, you can look at it as a multi-use area. For instance, in the story just told, we stayed in a one-room cottage, but it had areas split into sleeping, reading, cooking, working, and so on. This host knew how to divide the space to serve the purpose of each area in this small room. So, plan out your space accordingly.

The same holds true if you are renting a room in your primary residence. Can you fit a small desk and chair in the room as well as the bed? Is there room for a chair with a floor lamp for reading? Do you need to add a hanging wardrobe, or is there enough closet space? Make sure to add a mirror so that guests can get ready in their bedroom.

2. Scale and Balance

Another way to maximize the room's function is to create a well-balanced space.

For instance, creating an efficient layout requires using the right amount of furniture in the appropriate sizes to balance the space. Consider:

- If you overstuff a space with too much or bulky furniture, it will only make it seem overcrowded and small.
- If you have too little furniture, it can feel cold and empty.
- The fit of the furniture is also important. In other words, the scale or size of the furniture needs to be in line with the room size.
- Consider the proportions of each piece of furniture against each other as well as in relation to the size of the room. For instance, you wouldn't want to use a very large sofa in a small room or vice versa.
- Even adding a small desk to a bedroom creates functional workspace and is useful for travelers.
- The goal is to be minimal yet functional.

3. Space Planning

Guests will maneuver luggage through the space, so you need to allow for some breathing room between pieces as well as:

- What are the pathways that go in and out of the room?
- Is there an entry on one side and an exit to the outside or a path to another room? Be careful not to cut off those pathways.
- Design around unique architectural features like a fireplace or a big picture window with a great view.

4. Single-use or Multi-use Furniture

Whether you are designing a whole house or a small space, selecting furniture with various uses makes the space more versatile. Look at these examples:

- Bed frame with drawers at the bottom to store clothes
- Sofa that pulls out to a bed
- Ottoman used as a footstool or extra seating and doubles as a storage bin for throw blankets or games
- Table with a bottom shelf provides extra storage

5. Have a Place for Everything

When working with small spaces, you'll want to create spaces for guests to put their belongings. For instance, take full advantage of nooks or small spaces that can hold storage units. Utilize closets and shelves more efficiently by using bins, baskets, crates, and canisters to organize and store items. Make sure to add labels, so your guests can easily locate what they're searching for.

Here are a few more ideas for storing items:

- Open shelving
- Hooks on the walls
- Wall racks
- Overhead toilet ladder or shelving
- Closet organizers

6. Store Items Where They Will Be Used

To create a functional and efficient space, you want to group similar items together and store them near the area where your guest will be using them. For example:

- Store bathroom items under the bathroom sink or in the shower
- Store extra towels in the linen closet
- Store games in the living room ottoman

And my favorite is making the space in a kitchen more efficient. The key is to store items close to where they will be used. For example:

- Store pots, pans, and potholders close to the stove
- Put plates and glassware near the dishwasher
- Put silverware in a drawer below the cabinet holding the plates
- Put spices near the stove
- Keep mixing bowls, measuring cups and baking ingredients together in an allocated space

7. Remove Clutter

When designing your STR, use minimal pieces that do not clutter the space. As the saying goes, "Less is more."

Cluttered spaces impede maximum use of that space. For example:

- A vase of flowers on the bathroom counter reduces space for your guests' toiletries.
- Decorative accessories on the nightstands minimizes space for your guests' phones and glasses.
- Multiple appliances on the kitchen counter may make it challenging for guests to prepare meals.

Step 2: Desirable Design

Desirable design is all about the *visual* aspect of your design. This is what your guests will find appealing.

A functional design that has no visual appeal will be boring, so now we need to add in the visual part of the design process.

The visual design of an STR is similar to what you would want to see in a boutique hotel. You'd want to see something different from the four walls you're in every day at home. A beautiful, cohesive, well-balanced space with a great color palette will stand out and stop the scroll!

Desirable design includes a good mix of comfortable furniture and social spaces, colors, textures, nature, and light to let your STR shine in its own unique way.

Here are some tips on how to create an aesthetically pleasing visual appeal in a space:

1. **Identify a Design Style**

    If you haven't done so already, pick a design style or theme to carry throughout your space. Choose your style around the location of your property, the architectural style of your property, and the feeling you want your guest to experience.

    If it helps, think about words you would use to describe the space's emotional aspirations. Then choose the design style that matches that emotion. For example:

    - Warm—Coastal Mediterranean
    - Sophisticated—Art Deco
    - Elegant—Glamour
    - Cozy—Cape Cod
    - Dynamic—Boho Chic
    - Inviting—Farm House

    If you are not sure what these styles look like, you can get an idea by visiting: https://StyleMySTR.com

2. **Add Color and Design Elements**

    Create a pleasing aesthetic with the use of color.

    - Pick a color palette that coincides with the design style you have chosen
    - Start with a neutral base and add pops of color with art and accessories
    - Understand that color sells; lackluster doesn't cut it

- Continuity—carry the same design style and color scheme throughout the property

The character of the design will depend upon how these elements are used and combined:

- Add in different textures and touch-points
- Bring nature inside with pinecones, shells, palm leaves, and so on.
- Highlight features of the space
- Be cautious of putting too many knick-knacks around—leave space for guest's belongings
- Put accessories in groupings of three, in varying heights for visual interest
- Ensure everything flows and works together
- Think magical and memorable

3. **Furnishings and Accessories**

Once your design style is narrowed down, make a list of what furniture and furnishings are needed in each room. Plan with these tips in mind:

- Purchase sturdy and safe furniture, and if possible, avoid anything made of glass
- Chose things that will last—performance fabrics
- Always think about safety—make sure nothing will tip over or be tripped over
- Anticipate your TIG's needs
- Create social spaces
- Customize comfort as if it's your own home
- Make turnovers easier by avoiding unnecessary decorations
- Move sharp objects and breakables out of a child's reach

- Cover hardwood floors with washable rugs

4. Utilize Lighting Appropriately

Expertly placed lighting adds dimension to a space and brings your design to life.

Light draws attention to a space's textures, colors, and forms, helping highlight your design, no matter if it's daylight, mood lighting, or task lighting.

Ensure that your STR has the proper amount of lighting and wattage in each area. Consider the mood you are trying to create. The function of each room determines how much lighting or what combination of light is needed for that location.

For instance:

- Use brighter task lighting in the kitchen and home office
- Create a relaxed mood and atmosphere by adding dimmer switches to lights in a dining room or bedroom
- Use spot lighting for areas you want to highlight, such as a large piece of artwork, or a focal point in a room

Use a combination of ceiling fixtures, floor lamps, and table lamps. You may even want to add under-cabinet lighting in the kitchen for a dramatic look.

Step 3: Distinctive Design

Distinctive design is all about *styling* your space to create emotional connections.

Think of it as the pièce de résistance of the space. The wow factor. The icing on the cake.

Many designers think styling an STR is the same as staging a home for sale. In fact, they are quite different things altogether.

I know the terminology can be confusing so let me break down the differences between interior design, staging and styling:

1. Interior design is about *personalization* for a particular client.
2. Staging is about *depersonalizing* a home, minimizing a home's faults, and maximizing a home's best features so that it appeals to the widest possible range of buyers and helps the seller maximize the price and reduce selling time.
3. Styling helps prepare a home to look its best in images. The props used and how they are placed are meant to increase an *emotional connection* to the space and entice people to take action like clicking through, favoriting, sharing, or booking.

Styling an STR is similar to staging a home for sale, but there are some fundamental differences as well. As with home staging, STR styling aims to create a visually appealing design.

A major difference between staging and styling is staging a home for sale means that you do so in such a way that it will appeal to as many people as possible across a number of demographics.

But STR styling appeals mainly to your TIG rather than to the masses. You need a beautiful rental space that photographs well, is comfortable, and draws in those 5-star reviews.

Everything we have done to this point has been 100 percent targeted for your TIG; design and styling are no different. When your STR is styled for your TIG, your listing photos should resonate with them and encourage them to click through.

Distinctive STR styling helps you attract guests and contributes to a great experience for the guests while staying there.

Professional STR stylers are adept at drawing in potential guests' eyes. They are trained to understand the desired emotional state and how to create a vignette that will appeal to them.

With styling, you want to set a scene. Each room should tell a story. Think about vignette moments to bring to life throughout the property to help you stand out.

Here are a few tips for creating curated vignette moments:

- Draw inspiration from the local area, and have things align with events in the area or the type of location—present the local area through books, local artwork, and accessories
- Think of something they're not expecting; stop people and make them wonder
- Add vignettes—like a bowl of sand and shells on the coffee table if your house is close to the beach
- Match your environment—if it's an urban space, use graffiti artwork
- Match experience items with your location—such as framed music venue posters, if your STR is close to a thriving music scene
- Choose accent pieces that have character and start a conversation—even something small like a statement piece of art
- Hang mirrors strategically to add more light to the room
- Create a space that appeals to the five senses
- Differentiate yourself and be memorable
- Wow your guests

If you are sharing your home or sub-letting while away, make sure to swap out personal items for decor that's more on theme with the experience you're trying to deliver. Consider adding style to your STR with local artworks and fresh plants, rather than your own accessories and personal possessions.

SIMPLE SPLENDOR

A fabulous room is the creative combination of products, placement, and functionality at a price tag you can afford. The goal is to make your STR look and feel like a million bucks while staying on budget.

The best news is that whatever you invest in design will deliver maximum returns. Statistics show that when an STR is professionally styled, profits increase by 20-30 percent.

Although it's a good idea to refresh your furnishings every year and a half to two years, decorating in stages is also an option when working on a tight budget. Simply create a plan to allow the room to blossom as your budget allows.

Tip: If you want to charge premium rates, attract bookings that extend months into the future, and get awesome 5-star reviews, this step is critical.

Use Great Photos

Once your STR is designed and styled just how you want it, it's time to have professional photos taken to capture the essence and magnetize your TIG to you.

The phrase, "a picture speaks a thousand words," is absolutely true. Potential guests choose your STR over the competition based solely on your pictures and your description. The more your photos stand out, the better.

In fact, photos are the number one thing a potential guest looks at, followed by your description, so you need to grab their attention so they click on your property first.

But not just any photo will work. The secret is to take photos that evoke emotion.

Taking photos of the perfect angle of a room, or showing off the expensive artwork, is not the goal here. Your goal is to "stop the scroll" by making your space look different and incredibly attractive.

Understand that it's hard for people to imagine how they would live in your home, so you need to show them. Evoke emotion and create the feeling they are looking to have in your STR.

For instance:

- Put a novel and reading glasses by the bed
- Lay an open cookbook on the kitchen counter
- Set a big dinner table with decorative plates and a stunning centerpiece
- Set up a well-stocked desk with office supplies and a coffee cup in a well-lit space with
- Place candles and luxurious spa items beside a bathtub

Take it one step further and add lifestyle photos of people using the space.

Don't forget the exterior. The exterior provides valuable space for styled areas and will certainly increase your revenue. Consider these vignettes:

- Outdoor dining area on a nice deck
- Fire pit with Adirondack chairs
- Corn hole game with bean bags
- Hammock hanging between trees

Of course, you will also want to provide photos of your STR amenities, such as a pool or tennis courts. Also, take photos of outstanding views from the property, such as mountain views, beach views, views of a nearby lake, or golf course, as these are top STR sellers.

Once you have a full set of professional photos you are pleased with, you'll want to add creative captions and appropriate hashtags to each photo to give more information on the space. Tell your guest what they can do in that space. Help them yearn to be there.

Finally, consider taking seasonal photos and switching them out so that guests see what your place looks like in the season in which they are booking.

Implementing unique décor and professional styling and then capturing the emotional connection through photography will lead to more bookings and higher revenue.

If you follow each of these steps, you will find that your guests are much happier and much more likely to give you a 5-star review every time.

5-STAR HOST'R ACTION PLAN

1. Assess your property to see if it needs a refresh or a re-design.

2. If you plan on hiring a professional designer, ensure they are knowledgeable about the hospitality industry and have experience styling STRs.

3. Need help with styling your home? If you feel overwhelmed and design-challenged, I can offer you some professional help, including modifying your decor and furnishings so you can turn heads and attract more guests.

   For curated design collections where you can either purchase the whole collection or pick and choose the pieces you need, visit: https://StyleMySTR.com

   For help with e-styling services for STRs, visit: https://STRProStyling.com

4. For further training, check out my courses:
   - STR Design Course: StandOutBookMore.com
   - Direct Booking Website Templates: DiBSTR.com
   - How to Create a Welcoming STR Entrance Course: FrontDoorBlueprint.com
   - And more to come at: SubparToSuperstar.com!

Chapter 11

CONCLUSION

Well, we've come a long way together, and I hope you have found a few gold nuggets throughout this book that will help you rise above your competition. I hope that I have convinced you how vital receiving 5-star reviews is to your future success and your bottom line.

As you learned, the key benefits of reviews are to drive sales, build trust, and aid customer decision-making.

In the web-based world, 5-star reviews help build immediate trust, turning casual online visitors into paying guests.

In the travel industry, having 5-star reviews strengthens your hosting credibility and leads to a higher conversion rate.

I also hope that I helped you to see that 5-star reviews are not only had by luxury accommodations. All types of STR properties, in all areas throughout the world, can achieve the coveted 5-star review as long as they provide an outstanding overall guest experience. From booking through check-out, and everything in between, you must offer 5-star service. That's what hospitality is all about.

In fact, dictionary.com defines hospitality as:

1. The friendly reception and treatment of guests or strangers.

2. The quality or disposition of receiving and treating guests and strangers in a warm, friendly, generous way.

I trust that the stories and suggestions have shown you how important it is to be TIG-centric in order to receive that steady stream of 5-star reviews.

But before we part ways, I have a few final words to wrap this all up…

Differentiation will become more difficult as this industry becomes more saturated. To gain 5-star reviews, you need to be overtly aware of every step of the process for your guests.

So, again let me ask you the questions from the Introduction to see where you stand now that you have read through the book:

- Are you tired of sleepless nights wondering why you aren't receiving more bookings, more revenue, and more 5-star reviews?
- Are you fed up with trying to figure out the right strategies to get consistent 5-star reviews for your STR?
- Are you ready to set higher standards than the average host in order to provide your guests the best experience possible?
- Are you ready to step up your game and run your STR as a business that is TIG-centric in all that you do?
- Are you ready to join the ranks of the 5-Star Host'rs?

If you answered yes, then I encourage you to implement the lessons from this book into your STR business and join me in the 5-Star Host'r Movement.

The 5-Star Host'r Movement's mission is to improve on the STR industry. The goal is to change the landscape of sub-par stays and reviews. Every STR host has the ability to become a 5-Star Host'r by following the hospitality tips suggested throughout this book.

For your convenience, I have included "The 5-Star Host'r Principles" as an overview of the lessons you have learned. Make sure you print it out from page 36 of the workbook and implement each step to reach the 5-Star Host'r Status.

The 5-Star Host'r Principles

1. Get laser-focused to find your Targeted Ideal Guest (TIG). The riches are no longer in the niches; they are in the micro niches.
2. Become TIG-centric with everything you do.
3. Maintain good communication with your guests throughout their stay.
4. Ensure check-in and access to the property are easy.
5. Address issues promptly. Be available and reply swiftly when issues arise. Act as if the issue is more serious than the guest believes it is and solve it immediately.
6. Give your property a name and design your marketing around that.
7. Create a Branding Styling Guide.
8. Accurately describe your property and service offerings. Give the most amount of information with the least number of words.
9. Provide a House Manual with basic house instructions and refer guests to local businesses.
10. Ensure safety and emergency information is easily accessible.
11. Deliver flawlessly on service basics and essentials.
12. Differentiate yourself through emotional connection and alluring amenities that will enhance their stay.
13. Create a direct booking website at DiBSTR.com and keep updated on Web 3.0.

14. Anticipate your TIG's every need and provide an elevated experience.

15. Invite guests to engage in the fullness of your experience but respect their choice when they select other options.

16. Follow cleaning procedures after each and every stay.

17. Optimize the interior design in your listing to magnetize guests and make sure they are comfortable. Master your STR design techniques at StandOutBookMore.com

18. Style the property with vignettes, so your TIG can imagine themselves in the space.

19. Have professional photographs taken.

20. Create an experience that causes people to want to stay connected to you and/or engage with you frequently.

BONUS: ASK FOR REVIEWS!!

"We all need people who will give us feedback. That's how we improve."

~Bill Gates

Lastly, you may wonder if and how you receive the 5-Star Host'r title.

It's quite simple… once you have implemented the steps from this book and, in turn, receive ten consecutive 5-Star reviews—on any OTA site or your own site—you will be eligible to receive a certificate in the form of an NFT that cannot be copied or duplicated along with a copy of the digital badge.

Simply visit: 5StarHostr.com and follow the instructions to submit your reviews. Then your NFT certificate and digital badge will be returned to you within a week.

CONCLUSION

At this point, you will be permitted to post the badge on your promo materials, listing bio, or your own website, as well as purchase our merchandise that bares the prestigious 5-Star Host'r logo.

There you have it!

I hope you have enjoyed reading my travel adventures as much as I have enjoyed sharing them with you.

I encourage you to implement The-5-Star Host'r Principles and join the 5-Star Host'r Movement!

My greatest hope for you is that after implementing what you have learned throughout this book, you will join the ranks of the 5-Star Host'rs and thrive to the fullest!

Sharing is caring. If you enjoyed this book, please leave an excellent review on Amazon.

ACRONYM GLOSSARY

5-Star Host'r: A STR host who has upped the ante in their hospitality, design, and marketing to create a steady stream of 5-star reviews.

AI: Artificial Intelligence that leverages computers and machines to mimic the problem-solving and decision-making capabilities of the human mind.

COVID: Coronavirus Disease 2019

NFT: A Non-Fungible Token is a unique digital identifier that cannot be copied, substituted, replaced or subdivided, that is recorded in a blockchain, and that is used to certify ownership and authenticity.

OTA: Online Travel Agencies

STR: Short-term Rental—encompasses any STR whether listed in Airbnb, VRBO, HomeAway, etcetera, or your own direct booking site

TIG: Targeted Ideal Client

YOUR OPINION MATTERS!

Love this book? Don't forget to leave a review!
Every review matters, and it matters a *lot!*

I really appreciate all of your feedback and
I love hearing what you have to say.

I thank you endlessly.

Head over to Amazon or wherever you purchased this book
to leave an honest review for me at:

https://amazon.com/dp/B0BP45VT16

Thanks So Much For Reading My Book!
~Catherine DeGeorge

www.ingramcontent.com/pod-product-compliance
Lightning Source LLC
Chambersburg PA
CBHW060526100426
42743CB00009B/1439